The Speaker Author: Sell More Books and Book More Speeches

From my own experience, I can tell you for sure that a speaker who is an author will book more speeches, and an author who is a speaker will sell more books. Cathy Fyock is a master at helping you craft your book and market your book. Lois Creamer is a master at helping you market your speaking business. This book, *The Speaker Author*, is an amazing resource to help you take your speaking and authoring to new levels.

> — **Stephen Tweed,** CSP, Speaker Author, *Conquering the Crisis: Proven Solutions for Caregiver Recruiting and Retention*

The Speaker Author is a fabulous collaboration that addresses the specific needs of us all in this great journey of word-smithing! Whether you are a writer, speaker, coach, or consultant, this is the nudge and know-how that we need to move to the next step of influence through writing which promotes speaking which promotes our written words. WORTHY WORK... you will save this book and use it over and over again!!

> — **Naomi Rhode,** CSP, CPAE Speaker Hall of Fame, Past President National Speakers Association and International Federation of Speakers, Co-founder SmartPractice

Lois Creamer and Cathy Fyock are the dynamic duo when it comes to providing a clear roadmap to blending the worlds of writing and speaking. Offering clear, actionable advice for blending the two skills, Creamer and Fyock bring decades of experience from their respective fields. Whether you're a speaker who KNOWS that writing would bring added credibility or an author who wants to use the spoken word to push books out to an eager public, you'll find what you need in this easy-to-read book.

> — **Eileen McDargh,** CEO, The Resiliency Group, CPAE Speaker Hall of Fame, CSP

This book delivers on exactly what is stated in the title. If you want to book more paid speaking engagements and sell more books, then this is the perfect book for you!

> — **Shep Hyken,** Award-winning Speaker, New York Times Bestselling Author, *The Amazement Revolution*

It is a rare gift to be able to clearly, cleanly identify the path to success. This is a tool for every author, writer, and speaker's toolbox and bookshelf. I cannot recommend it enough.

> — **Melinda J. Kelly,** Author, *Finding Your Coach Diving Deep Within*

These ladies have spent decades, not merely years, collecting the insights and nuggets contained in **The Speaker Author**, and if you aspire to be a speaker and an author, this book will be a welcome addition to your shelf.

> – **Jeff Davidson,** Speaker Author, *Breathing Space*

Writing the book is only the first step. Leveraging your book into speaking engagements and increased sales is crucial. With Cathy and Lois's expertise in writing, speaking, and coaching they are the perfect combination to support any new author through the book writing and "what's next?" milestones. If there is a book in your head and passion in your heart, this team of experts is a must!

> – **Diane M. Rogers,** President, Contagious Change, LLC

In **The Speaker Author**, Cathy and Lois gift you their experiences in building a platform in a busy, distracted world. Once I got to the final page, I had more actionable ideas than from the last few trainings I've attended combined. This fabulous guide is a must-read for people wanting to take their message farther out into the world.

> – **Amy Luscher Smith,** Author, *My Faith Sparkles: Memoir of a Cancer Survivor*

Many years of experience and great expertise and tips throughout the entire book. Marketing at its best!

> – **Sandy Ringer,** President, Business Visions Consulting

As a professional speaker and author-in-progress, I'm happy to absorb every word like a sponge in *The Speaker Author: Sell More Books and Book More Speeches*. Cathy Fyock and Lois Cramer are experts in their fields individually, but collectively they provide a highly practical one-two punch for professionals who use speaking and writing as the tools of their craft. They deliver simple and powerful action items to demystify putting a book to work for anyone in the business of speaking.

> — **Elisa Hays,** CSP, President, NSA Northwest

Cathy and Lois have put their combined decades of knowledge and experience into this comprehensive book. It covers the whole range of issues regarding writing, publicizing, and selling your book. This is a must have!

> — **Dr. Jac Fitzenz,** Speaker Author

How do you get a jam-packed bank account from your book sales and speeches? Start by getting a copy of *The Speaker Author: Sell More Books and Book More Speeches*. It's jam-packed with proven strategies, ideas, and tips from mastermind authors Cathy Fyock and Lois Creamer. Each section offers an activity for the reader to apply what they learn resulting in their very own personalized plan to sell more books and book more speeches! As an author who is just launching a speaking practice, my investment in this book is money in the bank. I highly recommend it!

> — **Kathy Koultourides,** CPLP, Author, *Lucifer Leaders: The Hidden Cost of Deviant Behavior in the Sales Force*

As a new author, I have found a wealth of knowledge from the works of Cathy Fyock and Lois Creamer. Together, they have released a powerful combination of successful techniques for writing and speaking. *The Speaker Author* is filled with usable information.

> – **Gloria Sloan,** Author, *Abundant Faith: Secrets to Plenty Traveling on Life's Journey*

Every word matters – and I'm talking about the words we write and the words we speak. But finding the path to share those meaningful words with those who could benefit most from them can be daunting. *The Speaker Author* is the perfect book for those who have a message that deserves to be shared by providing them with strategic insights to be most effective. Whether you are an author, a speaker, or aspire to be either, this book is a must-have, chock full of everything you need to be successful in telling your story from the stage and from the page.

> – **Stephanie Feger,** Speaker Author, *Color Today Pretty: An Inspirational Guide to Living a Life in Perspective*

Speaker? Author? Speaker-Author? Absolutely! Cathy and Lois kick-it-into-high-gear with easy-to-follow practical tips and inspirational tools to get you started right now!

> – **Barbara Baron,** RDN, FAND, Nutrition Consultant and Speaker

Bring your message to life, as only you can, with industry insights from this powerful duo!

> – **Michele Lawlis Shelton,** Professional Speaker, Author, Coach, Consultant

Both of these extraordinary professionals have made me serious money by following their expertise in their previous works, **Blog2Book** and **Book More Business**. However, now these powerhouses have teamed up to help us speaker authors go even further in **The Speaker Author**. I can't wait to put these nuggets of wisdom in motion to increase my business and change the world!

> – **Stacey Oliver-Knappe,** Speaker Author,
> *The Customer Service Gurus LLC*

Cathy Fyock and Lois Creamer combine well-grounded writing and speaking advice with savvy pragmatism. This wonderfully presented collection of the ideas, systems, and processes they have used to run their successful businesses is a must-have for anyone who aspires to be an author and speaker. They cover the key strategic ways to use writing and speaking to build your business. It's said, "When the student is ready, a teacher will appear." Cathy and Lois teach you everything you need to know in this book.

> – **Rebecca Barnes-Hogg,** SPHR, SHRM-SCP,
> Author, *The YOLO Principle: The Ultimate Hiring Guide for Small Business*

Becoming a published author has transformed my business. My book has not only given me a platform, but I now have a higher level of credibility as an expert. My speaking and coaching business definitely has grown as a result.

> – **Vivian Hairston Blade,** MBB, MBA, PMP,
> Author, Executive Coach, Speaker, Trainer, Consultant

As a published author and an experienced professional speaker, I recognized some of the advice that Cathy and Lois share to be really effective practices I have used in the past. But, I still found a lot of great ideas that I'll incorporate into my work and business as a #SpeakerAuthor. There's something practical and useful in this book for those who are new to either side of the #SpeakerAuthor world, and something for those who are looking to sharpen their saw and learn a few new tricks!

> – **Mark Graban,** Author, *Measures of Success: React Less, Lead Better, Improve More*

Cathy Fyock and Lois Creamer are women on a mission. They, indeed, are changing the world one word at a time, whether they speak or write. Their book, ***The Speaker Author: Sell More Books and Book More Speeches***, overflows with their passion and commitment to offer the reader a book loaded with tips for speakers and authors. I highly recommend their book. It is a page-turner, and you may find yourself highlighting one tip after another.

> – **Yvonne Ortega,** LPC, LSATP, CCDVC, Speaker, Author, *Moving from Broken to Beautiful*® Series, Certified Speaking and Writing Coach

As the owner of a successful speaker bureau, I know the value a good book can bring to a business. Besides another revenue stream, a book illustrates the depth of expertise a speaker brings to the platform. In ***The Speaker Author***, Creamer and Fyock show you exactly how to use your book to grow your business!

> – **Betty Garrett,** CMP, Garrett Speakers International

As an author and book coach, Cathy understands the unique challenges that face writers today. She provides practical tools and exercises to help elevate their work, book marketing efforts, and author platform. *The Speaker Author* is not only for writers who wish to boost their careers and income through speaking engagements, but also for thought leaders wanting to learn the benefits of packaging their powerful message in book form.

> – **Sheila Manna,** Manager of Author Education, Author Learning Center

Accomplished professionals in their own right, Cathy and Lois break down the process of combining professional speaking and authorship into achievable steps. The "workbook" format of *The Speaker Author* combined with Cathy and Lois' easy-to-digest writing style make this book an indispensable "How To" guide in becoming a thought leader in your specific field.

Careful: This book may move you from "What, me write a book?!?" to "Let me tell you about my great new book!"

> – **Amy Brooks Hoffmann,** Fleur de Lis Photo Solutions

Lois sets the standard for speaker coaching. She knows how to get you started and how to keep you booked. Her model for positioning yourself is spot on. She's the real deal. It's worth reading the book just to get her ten questions for prospecting calls.

> – **Gerry O'Brion,** Professional Speaker, Author

Speakers love to speak and authors love to write, but when you combine the two, becoming a Speaker Author is an opportunity to 10x your business. Cathy and Lois have combined their expertise to produce a book designed to help readers leverage their knowledge to increase their market and message and generate additional revenue along the way. Who doesn't want that?

> – **Donna Hanson,** Certified Speaking Professional, Melbourne, Australia

Publishing has been my primary marketing tool and a key revenue stream for the past three decades. Fully 78 percent of our speaking, training, and consulting clients have come to us because clients saw the books in the store, got in touch after a media appearance, or responded to mailings from the publisher. This new book does a great job in laying out a practical path to speaker success.

> – **Dianna Booher,** bestselling author of 48 books in 60 foreign editions, including *Communicate Like a Leader;* and *Creating Personal Presence*

Wow! I've been a professional speaker and author for 29 years; I've authored 7 books; I've spoken for 800+ clients globally; I'm an inductee into the National Speakers Association's "Speaker Hall of Fame"—and I have never seen this topic handled better. Run, don't walk, to get this book!

> – **Karyn Buxman,** Neurohumorist, TEDx Speaker, Forbes Books Author, Member Speaker Hall of Fame

My first book created the single most significant boost in my career, and for the past 14 years, all of my books have been the greatest drivers of business for my speaking. Lois Creamer and Cathy Fyock totally 'get it' about the power of a great book for a speaker. Buy this book. Then write your own!

> – **Joe Calloway,** CSP, CPAE, Author,
> *Becoming a Category of One*

If you want to speak professionally ... if you want to book more paid speeches ... if you want to add the credibility of authorship to your speaking business, then buy this book and read this book, and most importantly, use this book. Cathy and Lois will accelerate your learning curve. They are the best!

> – **Major General (Retired) Vincent E. Boles,** Author, *4-3-2-1 Leadership*

Is your goal to increase your speaking business? In their book, **The Speaker Author**, Creamer and Fyock give you the proven strategies you need to use books to sell speaking which, in turn, will sell more books. Use this book as your primer on how to leverage your intellectual property.

> – **Susan RoAne,** Keynote Speaker, Author,
> *How to Work a Room* and more

Ready to book more? Start with this book. When two superstars like Lois and Cathy partner to create a body of work, expect a masterpiece! If you are serious about building your business this is a must-read for every speaker.

> – **Laurie Guest,** CSP, 22-year Veteran of the Speaking Business

Indeed, there are great speakers and there are great authors, but there are also a great many people who are missing out on the opportunity to strategically integrate these two components of a business and a brand. Cathy Fyock and Lois Creamer have individually perfected the art and business practice of being a "speaker author" – taking their messages from the stage to the page and back again, all for improved impact and profit. Now, in their no-nonsense, practical, and impeccable book on this topic, they have come together to share their experiences in a way that is sure to change lives and careers (and to delight readers and audiences). Each chapter contains a treasure trove of insights, activities, and do-it-now ideas that left me excited, energized, and ready to sell more books and book more speeches!

> – **Kate Colbert,** Founder, Silver Tree Market Research, Author, *Think Like a Marketer: How a Shift in Mindset Can Change Everything for Your Business*

If you are a speaker and subscribe to the widely accepted notion that "every speaker needs a book," then you really need THIS book. The authors are recognized experts on publishing and marketing for the professional speaking industry; so no matter where you are in the process, everything you need to know is right here. Writing the book is challenging. Knowing what to do with it is even more so.

> – **Keith Harmeyer,** Founding Partner, SmartStorming.com, President, Florida Speakers Association 2018-19

My one complaint is that Creamer and Fyock didn't publish this book in 1991, the year I wrote my first book. They would have shortened my learning curve by at least three years, and increased my income by probably half a million dollars. Do you think I can bill them retroactively for my losses?

> — **Greg Godek,** NYT Bestselling Speaker Author

Having a book is better than a business card. This must-read book is for speakers who want to prosper and authors who want to thrive. Lois and Cathy are the dynamic duo when it comes to booking business as a speaker and crafting a book that gets you booked.

> — **Pegine Echevarria,** Motivational Speakers Hall of Fame, SBA Woman in Business Champion of the Year, Florida

The Speaker Author

Sell More Books
and Book More Speeches

Cathy Fyock

Lois Creamer

THE SPEAKER AUTHOR:
SELL MORE BOOKS AND BOOK MORE SPEECHES

Published by
Remarkable Book Publishers
Louisville, Kentucky

ISBN: 9781092510783 (Paperback Only)

Library of Congress Control Number: 2019903934

Edited by
Ken Wachsberger

Cover design by
Randy Martin

Internal layout by
Amy C. Waninger

First printing, July 2019

Significant portions of this book first appeared, in some format, on Lois Creamer's Book More Business blog at
www.BookMoreBusiness.com/Blog
and/or Cathy Fyock's blog at www.CathyFyock.com.

Contents

1

2

Dedication

This book is dedicated to the National Speakers Association and its members. We love what you do for speakers and authors.

Acknowledgments

This book, like most books, has been a labor of love and involved an entire community of colleagues and friends we would like to thank.

First, we'd like to thank our amazing editorial board: Karen Lovett, Amy Luscher Smith, Cindy Hartner, Lisa Braithwaite, and Angela Greer. Thanks to you, the book is stronger and speaks to our readers' needs.

We'd also like to thank the many authors who have generously shared their books' success stories here, including Cara Silletto, Adam Calli, Fred Johnson, Eric Williamson, Peter Margaritis, Kate Colbert, Justin Patton, Stephen Tweed, Sara Potecha, Shep Hyken, Jeff Nally, Annie Meehan, Arlene Cogen, Mark Graban, Rob Campbell, Melinda J. Kelly, Brandon Smith, Amy C. Waninger, and Lee Quinn. A special thanks to Hayley Foster for her insights on TED Talks, and to Kate Colbert for her chapter to help us think like marketers.

Thank you to our editor, Ken Wachsberger, who Cathy met at the NSA Winter Conference. Thank you, Randy Martin, for the beautiful cover design.

We also want to thank the amazing Amy C. Waninger for publishing assistance.

Cathy and Lois are active in a variety of mastermind groups and want to thank these special friends for their support.

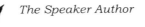 *The Speaker Author*

We also want to thank our family, friends, and our professional colleagues in the National Speakers Association.

You rock.

Introduction

If you're a speaker, you've likely been thinking that writing a book could be what you need to do to move to the next level. A book could help you book more speaking engagements, receive higher speaking fees, or secure more prestigious keynote spots. You believe that a book could be the ticket for more media coverage, more social media attention, or greater visibility with your ideal prospects.

Or, maybe you're an author of a nonfiction book, and you want to spread your book's message by speaking. You know that in speaking you can increase the profile of your book, and even sell more books in the process.

Sell more books and book more speeches

If either of these scenarios sounds like you, we're so glad that you've invested your time and money in reading *The Speaker Author: Sell More Books and Book More Speeches*. We believe that being able to speak as an author is a magical combination. But only if you know how to combine the two to create the magic.

As we'll illustrate, having a book alone is not enough.

I'm sure that you've heard of speakers who write a book and report that it did nothing for their speaking and consulting practice. You've probably also heard of authors who wanted to speak but couldn't somehow find those speaking engagements and opportunities. Having a book or a speech alone is not where the magic happens. It happens when you use your book and your presentation together.

In this book we'll share why the Speaker Author is an important role, and how to leverage each part to grow revenue. In Lois's work as a sales and marketing consultant for speakers, she has encouraged her speakers to author books as a sales growth strategy. She took that advice to heart when she authored her first book, *Book More Business: MAKE MONEY SPEAKING*, which is an in-depth look at how to grow your business as a paid speaker. She's already seen firsthand the magic that comes from speaking and having a book.

In Cathy's career, first as a human resources consultant and speaker, she knew the benefits of having authored books as she grew her business. Now, as The Business Book Strategist, she helps her authors write the books that will position their businesses for growth.

We are excited that you've joined us for this exploration of the Speaker Author role and how to maximize your impact. Because as a Speaker Author, you are uniquely positioned to make this world a better place by sharing your message through the written and spoken word.

About #SpeakerAuthor Call-Outs

Throughout the book we've added call-outs highlighting some of the book's key themes and ideas. All of them are Twitter-friendly and include our hashtag #SpeakerAuthor. We hope you'll join in the conversation on social media about the ideas you've found most helpful.

PART I.
THE BENEFITS OF BECOMING A SPEAKER AUTHOR

If you have expertise around a body of knowledge, you could build your business or your career if you were a Speaker Author. We work with many experts and thought leaders who have leveraged their intellectual property—their IP—and created more revenue streams, more visibility, and increased credibility.

For example, if you are a psychologist, a wealth advisor, an attorney, a CPA, a dietitian, or a physician, you have an area of expertise that you share each day with your clients, patients, and customers. But if you also wrote a book on your expertise AND began to speak about this topic at conferences and programs, you would likely grow your private practice and benefit from the revenue streams of speaking and writing.

In this section we're going to outline why writing a book is smart, why speaking is smart, and why authoring a book and offering presentations is brilliant! We'll spell out the benefits, and then, throughout this book, will share practical ideas and strategies for leveraging these two powerful tools to grow your business and career.

CHAPTER ONE

The Benefits of Writing

What can . . .

    . . . Open doors?

    . . . Elevate careers?

    . . . Double your revenue?

    . . . Create awareness?

    . . . Build excitement?

    . . . Garner publicity?

    . . . Change people's lives?

    . . . Illustrate the depth of your expertise?

If you had a tool that could do all that, wouldn't you call it "magical"?

Authors already have this tool: the magic that comes in writing and publishing a book!

But we must clarify. Just writing the book won't create magic. Books are like magic wands. They only create magic when they are used.

> *Becoming an author has catapulted my credibility as a speaker, given me the ability to raise speaking fees, and generated more revenue after my speaking engagements.*
>
> *#SpeakerAuthor*

Cara Silletto had been speaking for several years and wanted to move to the next level in her career. First, she wrote a chapter in *What's Next in Human Resources* where she shared her personal story as a Millennial in the workplace and found that her authorship credential helped her open doors for speaking opportunities. By authoring her own book, *Staying Power*, she was able to catapult her credibility as a speaker, raise her speaking fees, and generate more revenue after speaking engagements.

ACTIVITY

What are the three benefits you are seeking from becoming a published author?

CHAPTER TWO

The Benefits of Speaking

If you love to share ideas, if you love helping others learn, and if you love when you see the light bulb turn on for audience members, you know you're a speaker.

We are both enthusiastic speakers who love speaking, educating, and inspiring audiences. Here are some of the benefits that we value in this great profession of ours.

- **Increased visibility.** You have the opportunity to be in front of large audiences and are able to gain visibility with each audience member. Therefore, your potential impact is enhanced.
- **Increased credibility.** As the speaker, you have the power that comes from the platform.

You're the one on the platform—the spotlight is on YOU. You are in the limelight. You own the stage.

When you're speaking, all eyes are on you!

#SpeakerAuthor

You can excite people about your topic, your expertise. In speaking, not only can you share your passion and enthusiasm for your topic, but you can get others to see your point of view and join in your message.

There is a newsworthy quality of being the featured speaker at a conference. When presenting at a conference, the media may be interested in what you have to say.

Lois presented a program for the National Speakers Association a few years ago at their winter meeting. After her program she was approached by a columnist for *Forbes*. He liked what she had to say and ended up doing a column about her. Likewise, the business editor of her daily paper in St. Louis was in her audience when she did the opening keynote for Small Business Week. Within a week she was on the front page of the business section in the *St. Louis Post-Dispatch*. You never know who will be in the audience when you speak.

You learn as you continue to speak on a topic. Every time you present on a topic, you gain insights from the reading you continue to do on your topic, and from the interactions with your audience members. You can actually gain market intelligence by listening to feedback from them. Lois is a proponent of using pre-program questionnaires before a speech to gather information, so she learns more about the goals of the program, the demographics of the audience, and what specific problems they want to solve.

You're featured and quoted in conference publications. You receive media coverage and your comments are highlighted in conference publications.

You're paid for sharing your insights and ideas. Speaking is an excellent revenue stream in and of itself.

ACTIVITY

What is the benefit you enjoy most from speaking?

CHAPTER THREE

The Benefits of Writing and Speaking

If you are both a speaker and an author, the benefits are more than 1 + 1 = 2, since each one builds on the other.

You are in front of potential decision makers for presentations, consulting, and coaching, which leads to being in front of both potential individual buyers and bulk buyers for your book. As you share your philosophy and approach in your program and your book, you offer mini-sales presentations for your readers and audiences. As you build relationships with your readers and audiences, they see you as someone who can solve their problems. As you speak you build followers who buy your book who hire you to consult who hire you to speak, and so the story goes!

If you are both a speaker and an author, the benefits are more than 1 + 1 = 2.

#SpeakerAuthor

Speaking amplifies the power of your book, and your book amplifies the message in your program.

The book leads to sales and your speaking engagements lead to sales as you direct your readers and audiences to buy the next product in the pipeline.

Your book isn't just a product, and your program isn't just a product—each is part of your sales funnel that leads to larger purchases. A $20 book can lead to thousands of dollars in income!

ACTIVITY

Identify your primary benefit for combining writing and speaking.

CHAPTER FOUR

Quantifying the Benefits of Authorship

What would being an author mean for your speaking, consulting, or coaching business? Many nonfiction authors who write books about their areas of expertise discuss the intangibles of having more credibility or visibility, a larger footprint in the marketplace, or being seen as a thought leader.

If you had to *quantify* the benefits, what would that dollar figure be for your business? We have discovered at least four ways that authors might quantify the benefits.

Increase in closed sales: You visit a client. That client is on the fence or is considering another coach/consultant/ speaker. The client is trying to decide whether or not to choose YOU. What is the deciding factor? Would having a book make you the better choice because of your perceived value, your visibility, your recognition in your field? Remember, your book is your intellectual property on paper and positions you as someone with a deep expertise.

If you closed 10% more sales, what would be that dollar amount?

Increase in revenue streams: If you had a book, you could sell it at the back of the room when you were speaking. You could pre-sell the book before you presented your program. Visitors to your website could purchase your book. You could sell your book on Amazon. You could also develop other products based on your book, such as workbooks, discussion guides, or an online course. You could derive an entire revenue stream that you had not been generating in the past.

If you were able to receive 10% more in revenue from book sales, what would be that dollar amount?

Increase in fees due to increased credibility: You are considering raising your fees. Can you pull it off? If you are an author, you have more credibility and visibility, and the client may be willing to pay more for your services because of your increased perceived value.

Many authors report that having a book has allowed them to double their speaking fees.

#SpeakerAuthor

If you were able to charge 10% more for your services because you were seen as a thought leader, what is that dollar amount? Many of our author colleagues report that having a book has allowed them to double their speaking fees.

Increase in reach: Someone finds your book on Amazon, reads it, is impressed, and thinks, *I wonder if the author could come to our company and help us solve this problem.* Or, someone buys your book from you, lends it to a friend who has a problem with that issue, and suddenly you've just booked another engagement from a source you'd previously never encountered.

If you booked 10% more business because more prospects learned about your services through your book, what is that dollar amount?

Look at your revenue for the past year. If you could increase revenue by 10%, wouldn't that strategy be worth the investment of your time, energy, and money? And if you could realize a much larger return on that investment, would you even hesitate?

ACTIVITY

Calculate what adding a book could add to your current book of business.

CHAPTER FIVE

The Business Case for Writing

Sometimes our clients just say it better than we can!

In this case, Adam Calli, MSM, SHRM-SCP, SPHR, Principal Consultant, Arc Human Capital, LLC, and author of *Cultivating Culture*, sent Cathy this note. It exactly presents the case for why writing is such a powerful tool for building your business!

SPEAKER AUTHOR CASE STUDY

Adam Calli, *Cultivating Culture*

"What, are you crazy? I'm not a writer!" I thought to myself vehemently when I was first approached with the idea of writing a chapter for one of Cathy Fyock's anthologies. Sure, the idea of having the authorship of, at least a portion of, an honest-to-goodness published book to add to my bio sounded appealing. And, yes, I knew it would give me an added sense of legitimacy to set myself apart from the competition in the crowded market of the Washington, DC, metro area. I even knew it'd make my mom, grandma, and kids very proud! But really? ME? An author?

Then I met with Cathy. The first portion of my fears was alleviated when we went through the logistics of the editing and publishing process. But what about

---

21

the actual WRITING? Nobody could do that for me! Then she outlined the writers' workshops that would be offered which I could attend. She explained about the editing support that was included in the package to ensure that I would deliver a quality, polished finished product I would be happy with and would be proud to share. We also had a lengthy discussion about topic selection. By the end of our meeting, I was ready!

I've given my book to students in classes I've taught, to prospects, to current clients, to business partners, and I even donated one to my local library! I've sold copies of the book online (much easier to do than you'd think!) and after speaking engagements. I'm glad to have written my chapter and am exploring the possibility of doing another when the time is right. I can recommend Cathy as a partner to any author, whether you be an experienced author, or an apprehensive rookie like I was!

Also, my writing and PR efforts are really starting to gain traction! Guess who is quoted in SHRM's HR Magazine for the second time this year? Yup, if you said "Adam," you're right!

And I've been super fortunate to be quoted in two other articles on SHRM's website!

It's been a good year, and I credit writing my chapter as what broadened my perspective and introduced me to some new things that helped make this possible!

Finally, the "culture crew" [Adam's coauthors and cohorts in the DC area] and I continue to work together. We're doing a speaking gig for a local SHRM chapter, and we're continuing to develop our own ideas, and today we're having lunch. I feel certain that another article or two will be in the works.

CHAPTER SIX

Are You a Thought Leader?

A thought leader is one who is ahead of the trend, offering new insights and perspectives on an area of expertise. Thought leaders are often rewarded and valued for their ability to get in front of an issue and create a movement. Speakers and authors often see the benefit of positioning themselves as thought leaders since it's such a powerful business strategy. Are you there?

Take our ten-question thought leader quiz to see how you stack up.

1. Are you passionate about your topic/area of expertise?

2. Do you have a deep understanding of or experience with your topic?

3. Do you acknowledge other thought leaders and expand their ideas with your own experience and knowledge?

4. Do you offer a unique framework, a creative lens, or new perspective for solving problems?

5. Do you create new models, processes, or systems for a unique approach to an issue?

6. Do you use your own terminology and create new terms to define new concepts and become quotable?

7. Do you create a tribe or community with other thought leaders and followers?

8. Do you brand your ideas and concepts?

9. Do you explore divergent ideas and show similarities and connections?

10. Do you write and speak about your ideas so that others both understand and follow? Have you written your book?

If you scored between 8 and 10 "yes" answers, congratulations, you have arrived as a thought leader. If you scored between 5 and 7, then you have some work to do. And if you have less than five "yes" answers, you definitely are ready to up your game by using some of these strategies:

- Don't merely repackage the knowledge of other thought leaders; build upon their ideas. Read extensively from a variety of business and professional journals. Listen to TED Talks. Know how your ideas are similar to those of others, and how and why you offer a unique view.
- Share your passion about your topic with your followers. Explain why you are passionate about your work.
- Create your own model, process, system by using powerful analogies and metaphors to define concepts that are part of your brand.
- Create your own unique terminology to define your processes, systems, and concepts. Don't merely use the acronyms used by others.
- Don't quote others; quote yourself. Create sound bites that will become sticky.
- Create opportunities for conversation and connection with other thought leaders and those in your field. Ask questions on social media. Invite dialogue. Attend

conferences where your tribe gathers. Build your community.

- Speak and write about your expertise. Submit proposals to speak for your industry and professional conferences. Write blogs and articles. Publish on LinkedIn and in industry journals. And write your book.

Create sound bites that become sticky.

#SpeakerAuthor

Ultimately, you will become a thought leader when you write the book on your subject matter and claim it as your own. Then others will refer to you as "the one who wrote the book on it."

ACTIVITY

Take the quiz and see how you rank. Up your score by adding one of the action ideas shared here.

https://www.cathyfyock.com/the-speaker-author/

PART II:
IF YOU HAVE A BOOK
BUT AREN'T SPEAKING

If you've written your book but haven't been speaking and are hoping that your book will open doors for these opportunities, you're in luck! Your book can be a powerful tool to help you accomplish that goal. Having said that, note that we said your book is a "tool." The book, in and of itself, is unlikely to do anything for you unless you use it as a tool, just as a hammer or a screwdriver won't do anything without a little elbow grease and finesse.

In this section we'll discuss how you can begin to leverage your book to get the speaking engagements that you want. We'll talk about finding audiences (hint: think about your target reader) and connecting and negotiating with decision makers and meeting planners. We'll even review agents and bureaus as a strategy to book speaking.

CHAPTER SEVEN

How to Find Audiences

(*Hint:* Think About Your Target Reader)

Who is your targeted reader? If you've read either Cathy's or Lois's book, you know that your book isn't for every reader, just as your program isn't for everyone.

Lois tells the story of being approached by a speaker with a new program. After the speaker tells her about the program, Lois asks: "Who do you think would be a good audience for this presentation?" The speaker replies: "Everyone who wants performance improvement needs it." Then Lois suggests: "Go call everyone and see if they're interested." Obviously, this isn't a good marketing strategy.

Identify your target reader by as many characteristics as you can. Are they male or female? Young or old? Is this a book for business leaders, professionals, or staff? Will the book's content appeal to a certain industry (healthcare, manufacturing, retail) or a certain profession (human resources, marketing, operations)? Lois suggests picking an industry, then seeking out markets within that industry. For example, if financial services is your target, markets within that industry include banks, credit unions, mortgage companies, and accounting firms, as well as associations connected to each.

Also, return to your book's thesis statement (what your book is about) and consider the problem that your book solves. Does your book help organizations run more productively or efficiently? Do you help employees work better in groups? Does your message help people see the joy and beauty in everyday moments? Do you help organizations deal with change? By focusing on the problem that you address in your book's message, you'll be able to identify the right groups to approach.

Now, consider WHERE your ideal reader goes to hear more messages about the problem you solve. For example, human resources professionals are members of the Society for Human Resource Management (SHRM) and the Association for Talent Development (ATD), and therefore attend these associations' meetings and conferences. If your message is for women business owners, then they probably are members of and attend the National Association of Women Business Owners (NAWBO) conference. For professional women in business you might turn to the National Association of Women MBAs (NAWMBA).

Each of these organizations has national conferences and programs, and many of them also have state, regional, and local events and programs. While national programs may offer the greatest visibility, they may not pay speakers, with the exception of their keynoters (many of whom are celebrities or high-profile politicians). We've found that state and the larger city-based local chapters are excellent places to be paid to share your high-content program.

We like for beginning speakers to consider associations, since every time you present to one group you are reaching a large number of individuals who might hire you for a company program.

Consider presenting for both the state- and national-level associations. States typically have nine to ten meetings a year. National associations typically have one, and the field will be crowded with others who want to present. We've found that states typically pay a maximum of $5,000; national associations typically have higher budgets.

We think that it's smart to start with the markets you know and with which you are most familiar. For example, when Cathy started speaking, because her background is in human resources, she spoke for many SHRM and ATD conferences and programs. And, because she was an active volunteer with SHRM and had local, state, and national volunteer roles, she had a large circle of friends and colleagues who could recommend her to speak for their chapter programs and state conferences.

Never underestimate the power of relationships!

#SpeakerAuthor

Lois began speaking in two markets: to sales staff in professional service firms because of her expertise in corporate sales and marketing, and to groups of speakers due to her expertise in the speaking industry.

While you can do extensive research about prospective clients, we suggest that the fastest way to begin is by tapping into your network. By reaching out to your friend Jean in New Orleans you might be able to speak for the New Orleans chapter, and by speaking to that group you can get a referral for your next group, and so on. Never underestimate the power of relationships!

Also, a word on local versus out-of-town speaking engagements. If you're finding that booking local engagements for your full fee is difficult, you are not alone. There is truth in the scripture that you cannot be a prophet in your own land. We laugh and say that it is difficult to make a profit in your own land!

For example, Cathy was ultimately hired for her full fee in her hometown of Louisville, Kentucky, once someone from Louisville heard her speak for a conference in Philadelphia. Sometimes you have to start outside your local market to get paid for your programs within your local market. Lois wanted to speak at a large company headquartered in her hometown of St. Louis. When the decision maker seemed stuck, she decided to make a bold offer. She offered to fly in from Chicago if that would make him feel better. He realized how silly the situation was and ended up hiring her.

ACTIVITY

Identify three groups that could hire you based on your background and experience, and the problem that your book solves. Consider who you already know within this group and schedule a call to begin the dialogue.

CHAPTER EIGHT

I'd Like to Speak – How Do I Begin?

Speaking for conferences and programs can be an excellent way to boost your credibility and visibility, establish your thought leadership, and position yourself in your industry or profession. So how do you get started?

Get clear on your area of expertise and develop your topic. What are you passionate about? What do you do or know about that is nontraditional or unique? Do you have a new approach to share? Consider your unique area of competence and craft your message around this topic.

Create an outline. What are your key points? What does the audience need to know? What are the burning questions that they will undoubtedly have about your topic? Make sure that your content flows logically from point to point, and that you're not overloading your presentation with too much information.

Gather stories. There is nothing stickier than a story to engage your listeners. They will often remember your story long after they've forgotten your five key points or tips. First-person stories are great because they are unique and not duplicated by other conference speakers.

Create a strong opening and closing. Start your presentation with a story, a surprising fact, a perplexing question, or a quote that gets the audience engaged. Close with a call to action or a sound bite that attendees will remember after the program.

Listen to other speakers. When listening to other speakers, what draws you in? What engages you? Observe and adapt the best ideas to match your style and topic.

Give free speeches. Just as getting to Carnegie Hall involves practice, practice, practice, giving a great presentation also involves rehearsal. Offer to speak for groups that don't have a speaker budget to get experience before going into the big league. Make sure you get a testimonial every time you speak.

Just as getting to Carnegie Hall involves practice, practice, practice, giving a great presentation also involves rehearsal.

#SpeakerAuthor

Join a professional speaking group, and network with other professional speakers. Groups like the National Speakers Association can be a wonderful venue to meet fellow speakers and learn from professionals. For more information, visit NSASpeaker.org.

Hire a speaking coach. Through NSA membership, you can find a number of professionals who can help you hone your craft by providing you with one-on-one coaching.

Speaking for conferences, workshops, and programs can be a powerful strategy for building your professional brand, and long term can be an additional source of income.

ACTIVITY

If you haven't yet begun to outline your presentation, begin by sketching out your key ideas and identify your most powerful stories.

CHAPTER NINE

Lois's Ten Questions for Decision Makers

Over the years, Lois has developed ten magical questions to ask when talking with decision makers about speaking engagements.

Does your organization use paid, professional speakers?

#SpeakerAuthor

---

1. Does your organization use paid, professional speakers? This is a critical question, because many organizations use speakers but not all pay.

2. How is the decision made regarding speakers? You want to learn here whether or not the person you are speaking with is a decision maker, and the process involved. It may also give you a sense of timing and others you may need to influence.

3. Who have you used in the past? This may give you an idea of what topics they have historically used and how much they have paid for this information—a little market intelligence!

4. Do you have a specific meeting date set? It doesn't make sense to pursue this lead if you're already booked on the meeting date.

5. When do you begin to plan your meeting? Great to know when the meeting is, but important to know when plans are made so you can make sure you are talking to them at the optimum time for getting the booking. If now isn't the right time, you can put the follow-up date on your calendar or in your sales system (and call about one month prior to the time when planning is beginning).

6. Where will the meeting be held? Here Lois is looking to see if she may create some kind of competitive advantage for herself. For example, she lives in St. Louis. If the meeting is going to be in Chicago her expenses would be very reasonable. If they are deciding between Lois and a speaker in Los Angeles, she may get the job based on travel.

7. Is there a theme or focus to this meeting? How does the topic of your speech and book tie in to the theme?

8. Is there a budget I should be aware of? Here is the money question! It's important to get an idea about fees and budget early in the game.

9. What type of meeting is this? Is it quarterly, annual, semiannual? You want to find out how many opportunities a year this prospect may have to hire you.

10. Is there anything that I haven't asked you that you would like me to know about your meeting? This is a question to help you close the sale and add more value.

They will bring up any other questions or objections they may have.

The Speaker Author

If you have the answers to these questions you should be able to quantify how likely it is that you two will be working together or not.

ACTIVITY

We recommend you print these questions and keep them close to your phone when doing prospecting. You can download a template with these questions by visiting

https://www.cathyfyock.com/the-speaker-author/

36

CHAPTER TEN

How Do You Negotiate with Meeting Planners?

Of course, you'd like to make big bucks for every program you provide, and we've given you ideas throughout the book about how to make that happen.

But what if the client doesn't have any money? What if they are the perfect audience for creating future opportunities? What if you're not doing any other work? Shouldn't you be out making connections and prospecting?

There are a lot of times when you may waive your fee or provide a program for a reduced fee. Here are just a few of the ones we see:

- The client has NO budget because they've never hired a speaker before, but they might once they've experienced a professional speaker.
- The client is the PERFECT audience: They are the right demographic, they can hire you for future gigs, or you'd like to get their feedback and testimonials for future clients.
- The client is local, you don't have another engagement booked, and the event is close to today's date (so you're unlikely to get another opportunity for a fee-paid engagement).

Many times, though, you can negotiate, since there may be some alternative forms of payment that the client can offer you in lieu of a check, or in addition to a check.

Here are some ways you might be compensated for providing a program at a reduced fee:

- The client videotapes your presentation and provides you with a master that you can then use to develop your high-quality demo.
- The client has a prestigious name that will help you win other prestigious clients.
- The client offers referrals to others in the industry or provides testimonials that you can use in your marketing materials.
- The client promotes your presentation and will highlight you on their website with a link to your website.
- The client publishes your article or blog in their publication with a link to your website or with your byline information.
- The client purchases books for everyone in the audience, or for 100 of the first registrants.
- The client allows you to sell your books and products after the program.
- The client offers you a booth at their expo or exhibit hall at no charge.
- The client lists you as an in-kind sponsor and includes your name, logo, and contact information on all the conference materials.
- The client provides a list of all members or attendees and their contact information so that you can do a follow-up.

You get the idea: In addition to money, what can the client offer you that would offer value to YOU? Cathy likes to keep a list of these items handy so that she can easily negotiate when there is an economic reason to have this discussion.

In addition to money, what can the client offer you that would offer value to YOU?

#SpeakerAuthor

One of the strategies that Cathy employed early in her career was to help groups brainstorm about how they could pay her fee. For example, when working with SHRM chapters that said, "We typically don't pay our speakers," she would respond with options.

- What if, in addition to providing your noon keynote for your regular meeting, I also offered a workshop before or after the noon program where you could charge an additional fee and add value for your members?
- Have you ever had a sponsor for your meetings? Could we brainstorm together about who might be willing to have their name highlighted in exchange for sponsorship dollars?

In many instances, she was able to be paid her full fee and help the chapter bring in new members, offset all their expenses, and raise awareness for their chapter in the community.

One idea Lois has used is to offer an afternoon "hot seat" session that's about creating your own positioning statement. She's does this for National Speakers Association chapters and for other business associations.

ACTIVITY

Make a list of the benefits that the client could offer you that would be of value to YOU. Keep this list at your desk so you can use it when negotiating for your next presentation.

https://www.cathyfyock.com/the-speaker-author/

CHAPTER ELEVEN

Getting Started Speaking

If you have limited speaking experience, then you have some homework to do before you are paid to speak.

We highly recommend Toastmasters. For a small charge, you will learn presentation skills and story-telling as well as receive constructive feedback on your stories and programs. Lois calls Toastmasters "the off-Broadway of speaking." You may also meet other professional speakers. There are chapters across the country, and in many cities, you have options for breakfast, lunch, or evening meetings. Here you'll get lots of experience communicating in front of a group.

The next step is to get in front of groups with your program. Look for opportunities everywhere. A great place to start is your local business journal. It contains a calendar which lists any meetings taking place in the coming week, such as Rotary Clubs and other professional groups, and describes what their programs will be.

Call the group where you want to speak and ask if you can present your program. Don't be surprised if they give you 20 or 30 minutes. They usually do not pay; however, you want to ask for a testimonial letter from the leader of the group. We call testimonials "the economic capital" of your speaking practice. They are very important, and you should try and get one each and every time you speak.

---

*Testimonials are "the economic capital" of
your speaking practice.*

#SpeakerAuthor

When you speak without a fee, we suggest that you not use the phrase "free speech." Rather, use the term "waive my fee." Such as, "I may be willing to waive my fee in return for value other than money." This language is very important because it positions you as a paid, professional speaker.

Your next step is to leverage the testimonials you get into paid engagements. Remember that the people who hire you and pay you don't know whether or not you were paid for any presentation.

A great move now would be to see if there is a National Speakers Association chapter in your city or in a city near you. If you want to speak, you belong in NSA! Chapters are great places to gain expertise, meet other speakers, network, and befriend others who do the same work you do. You can find out all about NSA and its chapters at

http://www.nsaspeaker.org

Note: If you are new to speaking check out NSA's "Speaker Academy." It is designed to give speakers access to some of the best minds in the business via educational sessions.

ACTIVITY

Begin by assessing where you are in your speaking journey and take the next step. If you're just beginning, join Toastmasters. If you're honing your skills, consider the National Speakers Association.

SPEAKER AUTHOR CASE STUDY

Terry Chambers, *Rose Island*

I am a first-time author who has been developing a speaking platform since my book's release in February 2018. My book is historical fiction, based on an actual place—Rose Island on the Ohio River near Louisville, Kentucky.

In addition to the normal book clubs, book events, and bookstore appearances an author might be asked to be a part of, I was also able to create a brand new market to sell my books by developing a slide show and talk about the REAL history and events that took place during my book's timeframe.

Researching the book's background extensively allowed me to later develop a slide show and program that got me in front of a number of civic organizations, libraries, and historical and genealogical groups that would never have considered me if all I had to tell was the book's story. I didn't charge for any of these "mini lectures" but I was able to sell the book at every event and create interest in me as a speaking for future events. I have worked four or five events a month and currently have bookings for several more months.

As a result of all this activity and the reputation I am creating for having an educational and entertaining program, I have also been asked to head up an historical walking tour through the area I am using as the backdrop for my next book that is scheduled to debut next fall.

CHAPTER TWELVE

How to Respond to RFPs

Many conferences and programs use a process where speaker proposals are solicited from Speaker Authors. Generally, a Call for Proposals is posted on the organization's website or sent to their list of speakers and members anywhere from one month to more than a year in advance of the conference.

We bet you're wondering: *Are these a waste of time?* We have found that many conferences and programs are anxious to receive proposals from speakers they haven't heard before. Being both an author and a speaker may give you a leg up on your competition. Cathy and Lois and their clients have all benefitted from completing calls for proposals.

Ask if a fee will be paid to presenters. This may dictate whether you want to fill out the proposal.

In order to do these most productively, we suggest keeping an electronic folder of current topics and key information all in one place so that you (or a staff member) can quickly and easily complete these requests.

Typically, you'll need these essential components:

Session title. Have a punchy, compelling session title. Better yet, use the title of your book so that you can highlight your book in your proposal.

Use the title of your book so that you can highlight your book in your proposal

#SpeakerAuthor

Session description. Create a short (less than 100 words) description that is energetic and engaging. If you're not gifted at writing these, ask a marketing friend or professional to craft your message. You'll use this again and again.

Learning objectives. Write at least three learning objectives for your program. If the association or group has competencies, be sure to connect your objectives with their competencies showing how your program directly benefits their attendees and meets their needs.

Speaker bio. Craft a short (100 word) bio highlighting your credentials that relate to your audience. For example, Cathy is a former HR professional, and she highlights those credentials when applying to HR groups.

Picture. Use a current, high-definition, professionally taken photograph of you in your proposal. You don't want to show up for the engagement and find your decision maker looking for a much-younger version of you.

Link to a video or other proof of performance. Many conferences expect their speakers (especially keynote speakers) to have a current video. In lieu of a video demo, you may be asked to supply testimonials from other meeting planners, or a composite score from a past program.

References. In advance, ask at least three of your best clients to serve as your references for these proposals. You might also request that they post recommendations on LinkedIn.

The Speaker Author

Connection to their theme. If the conference or program has a theme (and many do today), then tie-in your presentation to the conference theme. If the conference has a carnival theme, then use a title with clowns or amusement rides. If the theme is about rock 'n roll, rock it out with your program's title and description. You'll be more likely to gain the attention of your decision maker when you tailor your proposal to meet their needs. Use the meeting theme in the subject line of all communications. This may actually set you apart from others.

ACTIVITY

Create a file with everything you need for responding to RFPs. Every time you add a new presentation or program, add this information to your RFP file so you can quickly respond.

CHAPTER THIRTEEN

Is There Someone I Can Hire to Sell Me?

Selling is hard. It takes time, effort, and a thick skin. So, you may be thinking, can't I just hire someone to sell me as a speaker?

There are several ways you might engage others to book you for speaking engagements. One is through speakers' bureaus, one is by hiring staff to sell you, and the other model is in a pay-to-play model. Let us review each one.

Working with Speakers' Bureaus

You may be thinking, *"How can I get a bureau to book me?"* The short answer is . . . you can't. Bureaus are interested in working with in-demand speakers—those who are getting rave reviews by delivering information in a compelling way.

If you have an in-demand speaking colleague with a bureau relationship, you may want to see if they might offer an introduction for you. Your colleague will want to have seen you and really believe that what you have to offer is a good fit for a particular bureau, since each bureau works with its own unique types of business and industry.

Some bureaus host "Speaker Showcases" and invite speakers to do 15 to 20 minutes of their best stuff in front of bureau clients and reps. Some charge for this; others do not. It is a great way to form a relationship with a bureau.

Some bureaus host "Speaker Showcases" and invite speakers to do 15 to 20 minutes of their best stuff in front of bureau clients and reps.

#SpeakerAuthor

Also, be aware that some bureaus will expect you to provide "bureau-friendly" marketing materials, meaning that your contact information should not appear on the material. The bureau wants the client to contact them, not you.

Bureaus ask for a percentage of your speaking fee as payment for getting you the engagement; the current average is 30%. In addition to paying the bureau a percentage, you are expected to promote the bureau during your visit and encourage the client to return to the bureau for future meetings. Also, audience members who hear you are to book through the bureau. This is considered "spin-off" business, and you are expected to contact the bureau and let them book the engagement.

Some bureaus even have "exclusive rights" or an "exclusive" with a speaker. This is the same as having an agent. It means all business goes through the bureau or agent and they take their percentage. Even if they didn't get the business, if you have an exclusive arrangement, you must run it through them. Lois suggests to her clients that they never agree to an exclusive arrangement without giving it a lot of thought. It will actually cause other bureaus to lose interest in you since they will be expected to split their percentage with the other bureau, and many don't think it's worth it. Further, no one will work as hard as you will to get business.

Lois always encourages her clients to work with a bureau if the situation presents itself. It's a great addition to your own efforts to grow your business, and you can learn a lot from bureaus about the business of speaking.

Hiring sales staff

Another question is, *"Should I hire someone and pay them a percentage of my fee to sell my services?"*

Lois discourages this type of pay arrangement for her clients. Speakers who pay commission-only will not have a very long relationship with their employee since it could be months before they get a booking. Why would anyone want to sell speaking services for you based on the promise of a percentage coming months down the road?

Success is not a solo act!

#SpeakerAuthor

The best scenario for a staffer? Pay an hourly fee to honor the other duties they do for you as well as a percentage based on your fee. If you want an employee to really stick around, Lois recommends offering a year-end bonus consisting of a percentage of what the business net profits are for the year. Doing this creates a staffer who is just as concerned with what is going out as what is coming in! You will have a real partner in your business.

Pay for Play

Some companies may offer you an opportunity to pay a monthly fee in return for leads. Lois's best advice? Forget it. Most of these types of businesses are in the business of collecting fees, not speaking engagements or leads! Will you get some leads? Perhaps. Lois suggests that you ask them to take their fee out of the first booking they procure for you. This will give you a good indication of how hard they would work for you.

The Bottom Line

The bottom line is that selling is difficult; but, most every successful speaker we know has at least begun by selling themselves. You learn what clients are looking for; you come to understand your value proposition more clearly. In short, you'll be much more informed when you begin by booking engagements first hand. Remember: Others may come and go. The only constant in your business is you!

ACTIVITY

Are you interested in exploring one of these sales strategies? If so, call at least three colleagues and get their best advice on what they've learned in using this approach.

PART III:
IF YOU'RE STILL
FINISHING YOUR BOOK

Maybe you have been speaking for some time but are now in the process of finishing your book. If so, you have opportunities for you to position yourself as a speaker in the narrative of your book. We've provided some simple yet powerful ideas to help you sell more books and book more speeches through your book content.

CHAPTER FOURTEEN

How to Write "About the Author" to Book Speeches

Fred Johnson wrote his book, *Five Wars*, because he wanted to tell his story, in both written and verbal form. He had been able to secure some speaking engagements and wanted to do more. When he sent Cathy his "About the Author" narrative, it included no mention of Fred as a speaker, of his high program evaluations, or that he'd won the Louisville SLAM. It would have been a terrible mistake to not position himself as a Speaker Author in his "About the Author" section.

What should you include in your "About the Author," and what shouldn't you include? First and foremost, your "About the Author" is NOT a detailed resume or curriculum vitae highlighting all your awards, accomplishments, and job titles. It needs to have relevance to your reader. What does your reader need to know about you in order to value your perspective and what you've brought to the table? A good place to start is with your positioning statement.

What You've Done

In this section, highlight ONLY those activities that are important to your reader. If the reader doesn't know what your credential means, then either omit it or explain it. You shouldn't give a blow-by-blow description of your work history but, rather, a high-level summary of the most important elements. Remember, when you try to attract interest to everything, you actually draw interest to nothing.

Remember, when you try to attract interest to everything, you actually draw interest to nothing.

#SpeakerAuthor

What You Do

The next section should include what you do and should give the reader an idea of how the reader might engage with you. Are you a speaker, a consultant, or a coach? List all of the vehicles you use to take your information—your intellectual property—to the market. How do you work with your clients? What problems do you solve?

As a speaker, you'll want to include the types of programs you offer, and perhaps name drop your most impressive client names. If you work with a specific industry or with certain professionals, you'll want to be clear about that work to the degree you want more of that work.

Connecting Points

We used to think that some of the "fun facts" were just fluff, but we've come to understand that these can be connecting points for our readers. Are you a dog person? Do you love opera? Do you play an instrument or speak another language? Have you lost weight? While not related to your topic, these personal attributes make you more real to your reader. Cathy often shares that one of her license plates says "QUEENB" and that Diane Sawyer's mother was her third-grade teacher. Lois adds that she works with Buddy, the Intern (her Labrador). When Facebook followers suggested she create a page just for Buddy she explained that, if she did, she'd have less interaction on her own page.

ACTIVITY

Create three lists: one of your most impressive credentials for your readers, what you do that helps your readers relative to this book, and some fun facts. Now create your "About the Author" using these three lists.

https://www.cathyfyock.com/the-speaker-author/

CHAPTER FIFTEEN

How to Sell Books Before the Book Is Written When You're Speaking

I'm giving a presentation before my book is released. What can I do? Eric Williamson, author of *How to Work with Jerks*, called Cathy to ask her this question. Here are some ideas.

Just because your book isn't yet published does not mean that you can't begin marketing it! In fact, there are many ways authors can and should get the buzz going well before the official launch. If you have the opportunity to speak for a group before the launch, why not maximize the opportunity?

Use the name of your book as the title for your talk. By using the same title for your presentation, you'll be strengthening the brand awareness of your book title. You'll also be setting up more interest for your book.

In your bio/introduction, position yourself as the author of the forthcoming book (title), to be released (date). Furthermore, include "Author of the forthcoming book" on your email signature for all your correspondence prior to launch. Many of our clients also proudly wear their "Ask me about my book" button to generate conversation at conference or program. Lois can attest to the power of the button to keep you on task!

Include "Author of the forthcoming book" on your email signature for all your correspondence prior to launch.

#SpeakerAuthor

During your presentation, make one or more references to the book. DON'T be a tease and withhold information to the group. DO mention that the book provides a deeper exploration into a topic or issue and share some of the content.

Provide a handout that includes your contact information. A handout may be in traditional format, or it could be a postcard, or better yet, a bookmark. Go ahead and create a mock-up cover (go to PowerPoint, and in portrait mode add a graphic, the title, and your name) and include this on the handout. Doing this allows those who hear you speak to be able to connect with you and potentially hire you for other speaking engagements, or to purchase your book.

Have some way for the audience to connect with you. For example, have a special white paper, checklist, or other handout of value that you send to attendees once you have their contact info. Attendees can access this "Irresistible Free Offer (IFO)" by visiting a landing page. Or, use a response card that attendees complete with their contact information, and request any of the IFOs mentioned in the program. You may also use electronic means to gather information, with programs like kiwilive.com. The speaker asks audience members to text "IFO" or a keyword the speaker chooses (for example "Lois info") and the offer is immediately provided and contact information received.

Pose a question or issue that has people talking to you or about you during the conference that is connected with your book. Invite people to share a story with you or use a catch phrase that is repeated or shared during the conference. For example, with Eric's book about working with jerks, he asked for examples of jerk stories and was able to gather several new stories for future blog posts.

Offer a "deal" to people who respond to a "pre-publication" offer of the book. Maybe attendees can pay now and get an autographed book with free shipping. If you offer pre-publication sales, be transparent with your customers about launch dates and keep them posted on publication details. Many have used this strategy to actually fund creation of their books!

SPEAKER AUTHOR CASE STUDY

Peter Margaritis, Taking the Numb Out of Numbers

One of our favorite stories of how to promote your book when you don't have actual books on hand was demonstrated by our friend Peter Margaritis, author of *Taking the Numb Out of Numbers*. He was scheduled to attend Influence, the annual convention of the National Speakers Association, and wanted to let his friends and colleagues know about his new book. The problem was that the book would not be available until after the convention. Not wanting to miss an opportunity, Peter, with the help of his publisher Kate Colbert of Silver Tree Publishing, created large postcards the size of his book, with the book's cover on one side and other

---

book details on the other. Throughout the conference Peter and his author friends posed holding the book (the postcards) and created buzz on social media. The strategy worked so well that when Kate Colbert's new book, *Think Like a Marketer*, was released, she also created postcards and continues to sprinkle these when attending meetings and appointments, making others aware of her excellent new book.

Kate adds, "Perhaps key to that story is that both of us had our books already available for pre-order on Amazon at the time we promoted our books via the postcards, so we were able to "close the deal" on the interest we drummed up with the cards because the cards were more than just a buzz-generator or a 'coming soon' announcement. The cards were the coming-out party for the books — a sort of 'Did you know about my new book? Here's the scoop and a photo. Here's how to pre-order your copy today. Thank you.'"

ACTIVITY

Just because your book isn't finished does NOT mean you can't begin promoting it in your next presentation! Consider one of the ideas provided here to include in your next engagement.

CHAPTER SIXTEEN

How to Use *"Author of the Forthcoming Book"* to Position Your Speaking Business

Your book may not be completed, but there is no reason you can't begin promoting your book by using "Author of the forthcoming book" in a number of creative ways to generate buzz and excitement, and even capitalize and leverage the book's launch for your speaking business.

Use in your speaker introductions. As part of your speaker introduction (and bio, for that matter) include "Author of the forthcoming book" with the book's title.

Create cover art before the cover is done. Even if you still have only a working title and a cover you've mocked up in PowerPoint or other design software, use the cover art to make your book more real and tangible.

Ask for feedback on your book's cover on social media. Several authors we've worked with have offered their two favorite cover designs on social media to garner early interest for the book, and to create buy-in and community around the book.

Use on email signature. Proudly state that you are "Author of the forthcoming book" with the cover art. We've known several authors who have pre-sold books and booked speaking engagements based on just this one simple idea.

Proudly state that you are
"Author of the forthcoming book"
with the cover art.

#SpeakerAuthor

Mention in speaking presentations. During your presentation, make mention of your new book and cite some new research or insights that you'll be sharing. You'll not only be giving them a "sneak preview," but you'll also be creating interest. You might even have a sign-up sheet or use response cards to identify those who would like to pre-order books.

Include in your byline on all articles and blog posts. As you're writing blog posts and articles on topics related to your book's theme, add "Author of the forthcoming book" to your byline along with your contact information.

Preview content from your book in your blog and on social media. Speaker Author Justin Patton generated interest on social media for his new book, *Bold New You*, by premiering excerpts prior to the book's launch. He enticed Cathy to follow his link and pre-order his book on Amazon.

Include it on your one-sheet. If you have a working title for your book, include it in your Speaker Author one-sheet. Include cover art as soon as it is available (even a mock-up).

Wear your magic button. Wearing a button that says "Ask me about my book!" is advertising that you are the author of your forthcoming book. Wear your button when traveling, networking, and whenever you'd like to generate interest. Cathy has also created removable laptop and cell phone stickers with the same message.

ACTIVITY

Create a mock-up of the book's cover and select one or more of the items on this list to implement NOW.

CHAPTER SEVENTEEN

How to Use Your Book's Narrative to Generate More Speaking Engagements

There are many ways you can generate more speaking engagements and spin-off business within your book's narrative.

For example, you might include some phrases that let the reader know you are a speaker and that you regularly provide programs on this and similar topics. While it may seem obvious to you that you would like to do more speaking and spin-off engagements, readers may not be aware and are only given this idea when you mention in your narrative that you do other presentations. Do this by including phrases such as the following:

- When I was speaking for XYZ organization . . .
- In my workshops, attendees usually ask me . . .
- One of the problems faced by your industry was voiced when I spoke with . . .
- Here's a great example that was shared at a recent program . . .
- When working on a complex consulting assignment solving the problem of . . .
- During a coaching engagement, I heard this . . .

- In one of the assessments I use, I found that . . .

Another idea is to include exercises or discussion questions at the end of each chapter or section and include language that lets readers know that you can also facilitate these learning sessions in their organizations.

As you're writing your book, get permission from clients and use their case studies in your book.

#SpeakerAuthor

As you're writing your book, get permission from clients and use their case studies in your book. You are now demonstrating to your readers the work you've done for other clients. Or, you might ask clients to write up their experiences for you to include in the narrative or as a boxed text. Or our favorite idea is to interview clients or, better yet, potential clients for examples to use in your book. Your call is no longer as a speaker looking to book an engagement, but as an expert looking for more content to highlight in your book. Many potential clients will be flattered by your request and see this as an opportunity to help position them or their companies. They can help you build a relationship quickly that could lead to consulting or training assignments.

ACTIVITY

Review the book's manuscript and determine key places to add some of these positioning strategies. Or, if your book is already complete, use these strategies in blogs and articles that you write to continue to position yourself as the "go-to" expert.

CHAPTER EIGHTEEN

How to Pre-sell Books on Amazon

Amazon pre-sales occur when customers can go on Amazon and place an order for your book before it is ready for sale. So, while you're putting the finishing touches on your book, getting those last-minute endorsements, or fine-tuning a chapter, you're able to rack up sales through Amazon.

Is it important to offer your book for pre-sale on Amazon?

Yes! There are a number of reasons why Amazon pre-sales make so much sense:

- You're able to move from "forthcoming book" to "available for pre-sale now," which makes your book real for both you and your audiences when you speak.
- You're able to capture the impulse sale when you speak! When you speak before the book is ready, this pre-sale feature allows for your audiences to buy your book immediately.
- This is a great strategy for busy authors and allows you to promote your book long before the book is officially released.
- It takes the pressure off! You want to publish a professional volume but DO have a sense of urgency to get it done!

And, last but not least—the biggest reason of all—by aggregating sales from all the pre-sales to your first official launch date, you're better able to position your book as a bestselling new book in its category. Yes, it's a bit contrived, but you can use this tagline in your future one-sheets and promo materials.

How to Make Your Book Available

- Discuss with your publisher. Most large publishing houses already do this for their clients, but you may need to request this service if you're using a hybrid or self-publishing option.
- This feature is already available for eBooks; you'll need to request the option for print-on-demand books.
- Ideally, you'll want to make this offer four to ten weeks prior to the official launch; you don't want your readers to put their money down and wait too long before they receive their books.

Tips for Making Your Book Available

Because Amazon Advantage is not open on nights and weekends, Kate Colbert of Silver Tree Publishing suggests that you not attempt this on a Friday. If you have a glitch it will be Monday before your issue is resolved.

ACTIVITY

Talk with your publisher to see if you can make your book available for pre-sale on Amazon.

PART IV: WHEN YOU'RE SPEAKING

You've booked the speaking gig. Now, how do you maximize this opportunity? Books don't magically sell themselves, and audience members don't necessarily think about helping you book your next speaking engagement unless you take some specific actions. In this section, we'll explore how to make book sales before, during, and after the engagement. We'll do a deep dive into how to build back-of-the-room sales and generate bookstore sales. Most importantly, we'll share some insights about how to send messages to audiences that position you as their next speaker!

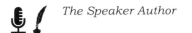

CHAPTER NINETEEN

Bulk Sales and Packages

One of the best ways to sell books and increase the revenue you obtain from any speaking engagement is to sell your book in bulk when you book the speech.

Let's say that XYZ organization has just booked you for their upcoming conference. As you are gathering the details for the engagement and before you finalize the deal, ask one of these powerful questions:

- "Do you think it would make sense if your attendees had a way to continue learning after the event?"
- "Do you think it would make sense for everyone in the audience to be able to walk away with a companion book to this program?"
- "Would you be adding more value if each attendee walked away with my book to reinforce the learning?"
- "Would you be able to attract more attendees by offering a book to each person?"
- "Do you think it would make sense for your group to be able to walk away with more information than I'll have time to share today?"

These questions are magical, in that they position you and your book as a powerful value-add.

And, if you've been able to arrange a publishing deal that allows you to buy books at cost, you can even offer the decision maker a nice discount to have attendees walking away with a book in their hands. For example, if you buy your books at $5 each and they sell for $20, you can offer pricing at $15 or $18 per book and realize a nice profit on top of your speaking fee (or in lieu of your fee if you're just starting out). Or, you might offer a discounted speaking fee but charge full price for the books (some organizations have a "materials" budget but have a small "speaker" budget). The opportunities are endless.

> *"Would you be adding more value if each attendee walked away with my book to reinforce the learning?"*
>
> *#SpeakerAuthor*

Speaker Author Shep Hyken offered customized covers and title pages to his clients. He has printed runs of the book with the customer's logo on the front saying, "Special edition for the XYZ Company," and for associations, "Special edition provided by the XYZ Association for its members."

Add Book Sales to Your Event Sales Process

SPEAKER AUTHOR CASE STUDY

Cara Silletto, *Staying Power*

We've built book sales into our event sales process and emphasize it as a value-add option before closing any contract. We offer bulk discounts and the option to ship the books direct to the client ahead of time, so they can be included in attendee bags or set out on the day of the event. And there are key incentives for both corporate and association clients to use this option.

For corporate event planners, purchasing the book for their group helps get attendees on the same page and keeps the momentum going even after the event is over. With associations, we encourage the win-win scenario of getting a vendor to sponsor the book purchase which increases the vendor's visibility and makes the association look good for improving the takeaway value of the conference for attendees.

Although you may still need to use the book table for most of your clients, you only have to presell to a couple of events before you'll see significant growth in overall book sales.

One other way our book helps support our client relationships (and vice versa) is by helping us stay connected with our audiences long after our events have ended. Once a conference or a workshop is over, it's easy to move on and forget the momentum or inspiration of the moment. Not only do attendees stay connected to our message by reading the book, they also discover we've included a link to a hidden webpage that offers post-reading group discussion questions, free resources, and options to interact with our team. Our readers have loved this and it's led to additional touch points with prospects we probably would have lost touch with otherwise.

Create Custom-Branded Books for Key Customers

SPEAKER AUTHOR CASE STUDY

Stephen Tweed, Conquering the Crisis: Proven Solutions for Caregiver Recruiting and Retention

The simplicity and speed of Print on Demand (POD) makes it easy to create custom-branded editions of your book. An idea that came up during a conversation with my publisher was to create a new edition for one of my best clients. The client wrote a short one-page Foreword for the book. The publisher created a new cover with "Foreword by ... <Client's Name>" on the front just under my name.

We pre-sold several hundred copies of the book to the client and had them printed and shipped ahead of the client's meeting. On the day of the meeting, everyone received a copy of the book in their packets. The client introduced the book when she introduced me as the keynote speaker.

After the speech, we had a book-signing table set up where I autographed books and put an "Autographed Copy" sticker on the cover.

Another client who owns a software company that is specific to our niche market asked me to do a webinar for her customers. I quoted her a fee and offered to create a custom book with her Foreword. She loved the idea. We designed and printed the books and shipped them to her office.

She planned, organized, and promoted the webinar. We did the webinar in an interview format with her asking the questions. Then she sent a copy of the book to everyone who registered. She later came back and purchased more books.

Now, whenever I'm talking with a prospect about a speaking engagement, I discuss the custom book option. Many of them love the idea. Not everyone wants to do it. Some just buy the regular soft-cover edition. Others choose not to pre-purchase books but allow me to sell them in the back of the room.

I've found that audience members really love having a book with the Foreword by their CEO, and personally signed by me with an autograph sticker on the front.

SPEAKER AUTHOR CASE STUDY

Sara Potecha, West Point Woman: How Character Is Created and Leadership Is Learned

Early on as a first-time author, I was told that the income from my book sold on Amazon would be very small per book and I would need to wait patiently to be paid quarterly. Being an unknown writer, the idea of selling a huge number of books on Amazon was unrealistic. Instead, the real revenue is found in booking speaking engagements and then possibly selling a few books on the side. Becoming an author, however, gave me credibility when breaking into the speaking business. This was all good, sage advice; however, I discovered another way of generating income through a high volume of books sales sold directly to a client while also securing a speaking gig.

And to be forthright, I learned this technique from one of the leaders of the National Speakers

Association (NSA) Military/Veteran Connection group. My fellow veteran suggested that I offer a special edition copy of my book to a client when negotiating about a speaking gig. A special edition copy, he explained, involves having the CEO or President of the company/organization read the book and agree to write a Foreword. Having worked in the corporate world for many years, I realize in some cases the CEO may not actually read the book and his/her Communication staff may actually pen the Foreword. Yet, the idea is to get the organization to see value in having a specialized copy of the book and to simply agree to compose a short one-page Foreword. Then in working with my publisher, we remove the original Foreword and replace it with the client's CEO/President's copy. We also add the client's logo to the book cover.

The benefit to the client is that they get a personalized copy of the book to gift to their employees and/or customers; and because of the specialization, they often will buy hundreds of copies of the book. Further, a special edition copy of the book is another means of extending the client's brand. The benefit to an author is not only the revenue generated from a large number of books sold and the potential number of people reading your tome, but that you also gain another endorsement of your book, that of the client's CEO or President. Those endorsements can then be added to your website and social media platforms and used as a reference when submitting proposals for higher-paying speaking events.

Recently, I used this technique with a long-time client who purchased 500 copies of my book. I discounted the book from $19.95 to $15.00 a book; incredibly the client loved the idea so much, they paid for the order upfront! They also hosted and catered my book launch event and in exchange I gave a 40-minute keynote speech based on my book. The set up for the special edition copy cost me about $600 and there were some minimal shipping fees, yet the event netted me well over $5000 – not bad for 40 minutes of speaking and a catered book launch where well over 300 copies of the original copy of the book were also sold!

Currently, I am working through the details with a new client purchasing 1700 copies of my book! As a first-time author, selling that many books on Amazon could take years! I believe giving a substantive item like a book appeals to many clients since a speech is just that: 30 to 50 minutes of talking, even if delivered brilliantly, that will still soon be forgotten. A book, however, is tangible – a gift that keeps on giving as it can be referred to over and over again.

Authors, offer special edition copies of your book and earn more revenue!

ACTIVITY

Identify your clients who would value and use your book in bulk. Make calls to your top clients and discuss this option.

CHAPTER TWENTY

How to Sell Books While You Speak

A few years ago, Cathy attended a conference featuring women authors. Exciting event. Diverse authors. Great presentations. So many lost opportunities!

All these speakers/authors had a fabulous opportunity to build their fan/reader base, yet almost none of them took advantage of these easy tips for maximizing the marketing benefit of speaking about their books at a conference.

In the conference program, include the name of your book as part of your session title. This makes your audience members see the book as a souvenir of their experience. As one speaker told us, "They were so engaged in the presentation that they want to take us home."

Be sure your introducer uses the name of your book by giving them your introduction in advance and taking an extra copy of your intro to the conference. (Note: Cathy keeps a laminated copy of her introduction in her packed luggage so she's always ready!) Be sure to let your introducer know that you are doing a book signing after your session and ask that person to mention it when you are introduced. Then ask your introducer to remind attendees at the end of the session to join you in the bookstore (or back of the room) immediately following your session to buy your book.

Mention the name of your book throughout your presentation. State the title slowly and distinctly; you know it so well, but your audience doesn't.

Mention the name of your book throughout your presentation.

#SpeakerAuthor

Offer a handout, postcard, or bookmark as a takeaway that includes your book's name and how to reach you (via email, telephone, Facebook, Twitter, LinkedIn). Your readers want to be able to connect with you so don't make them search. Bookmarks are especially good for authors since they brand you as a Speaker Author, and they are relatively inexpensive.

Read from your book and HOLD A COPY OF YOUR BOOK! Even though you may have it electronically and can read it from your phone or other electronic device, it is powerful to hold the book and let the audience see the cover of your book. One of the keynote authors at this conference read from her phone and lost the entire opportunity for us to see her book cover and take pictures with her holding her book (a branding opportunity). At least once, say, "As I discuss in my book . . ." and provide the information.

Don't tease attendees or withhold information when speaking. A definite no-no is saying something like, "I would answer that question, but you'll need to buy the book to get the answer." This is always wrong. Instead, you might say something like, "If you'd like a deeper dive on this issue, you can find it in my book or I'm happy to talk offline" (after you've answered the question in a general way).

Have a method to collect the names of those attending your session. You can do this by having a sign-in sheet ("sign-up for my free newsletter or blog"), collecting cards and giving a door prize (like your book!), or by offering a free goodie (like a sample chapter or other tangential product). You can do this by asking attendees to send an email to you or to visit your website to download the freebie (in marketing we call this freebie an "irresistible free offer" or IFO).

There are electronic ways to capture contact information. One that many speakers use is KiwiLive.com. This allows audience members to text you for your free offer. When they do, the offer can be automatically sent, and their contact information captured. It's so easy!

During your presentation, mention your website and your IFOs (give them a reason to visit your site!). You want readers to engage with you! This is a great way to get signups for your blog.

Use a PowerPoint or poster that includes the cover of the book and its title and your contact information. If you want to encourage Tweeting during your presentation, share your hashtag by announcing it at the beginning of your presentation or on your PowerPoint.

Offer your books for sale after you speak and be sure to announce when and where your book signing will be. Be sure that the conference planners allow plenty of time following your session for individuals to purchase your book. Ideally, position the bookstore close to your conference presentation site, or set up a sales counter outside your speaking venue. Ask anyone wanting to ask you questions after the program to join you in the bookstore (or walk with you).

When you sign your books, be sure to get a card or contact information from your reader (which makes it easier to personalize their books, too!). Offer to personalize your book for the reader and offer a bookmark or label for the book that says, "Autographed by the author."

Take pictures of you holding your book with those who have purchased your book. Post these on social media and share the post with your new readers.

ACTIVITY

Create your own checklist for preparing for speaking engagements that includes the important elements here! Get started with a template at:

https://www.cathyfyock.com/the-speaker-author/

CHAPTER TWENTY-ONE

How to Sell Books After You Speak

When speaking for larger association conferences, you may have the ability to place your book in the conference bookstore. Here are some suggestions for making the most of this opportunity.

Ask if the conference or program offers a bookstore. Not all conferences have a bookstore program, and each is run a little differently. For example, for several years Cathy has run the conference bookstore with her colleague Jeff Nally for the KY SHRM Conference. Fifty percent of the Speaker Author book sales benefit the SHRM Foundation. Cathy sends out a notice to all the selected speakers to determine if they are interested in offering their books for sale.

Know the terms of sales/returns. Most bookstores will provide 50% of proceeds to the author but be sure to ask about the specific terms of sales and returns. Is it your responsibility as the author to take back unsold books? You may want to work with your publisher for the best arrangements.

Come early and stay late. Speaker Author Annie Meehan is a pro at maximizing her book sales. When keynoting for a conference, she often comes early and stays late so that she can develop relationships with the attendees and other speakers. She brings attendees with her to the bookstore, so they can buy her books. She offers fellow speakers a book as a gift. She takes selfies with her newfound friends.

Ask your introducer to mention your book-signing hours at the bookstore and remind attendees again at the end of the program. This allows you as the author to not directly sell from the stage (a no-no for many conference programs).

Promote your presentation. Does your tribe know that you're speaking at the conference? Let them know in advance through your newsletter or social media, or by videoing a short promotional clip about your session. Let attendees know that you'll also be at the bookstore for your signing. Some speakers make up postcards or bookmarks that promote their workshops or keynotes and book-signing times and give these out throughout the conference to generate more interest. Your clients will love you for doing this.

Make Your Books More Valuable When You Autograph

SPEAKER AUTHOR CASE STUDY

Stephen Tweed, Conquering the Crisis: Proven Solutions for Caregiver Recruiting and Retention

You can make your book more valuable to people who buy them at the back of the room after a speech, or pre-purchased books you sign at the back of the room, by writing a personal message and adding an "Autographed Copy" gold sticker.

I'm surprised how many Speaker Authors sign books with a simple scrawl that is not recognizable as their name, and who don't use autographed stickers.

81

Think of a short message that has meaning for the reader. When you sign books, write that short message, and sign your name legibly. It means more to the reader and they tend to keep your book on their desk or on their bookshelf. Having your signed books visible keeps you in the front of mind and creates opportunities for referrals.

My most recent book is Conquering the Crisis: Proven Solutions for Caregiver Recruiting and Retention. When I sign the book, I write ...

"Keep your focus on Conquering the Crisis"

Stephen Tweed

(Date)

It takes a few seconds more than a simple signature, but it makes it much more personal and adds value to the book. Adding the date after my name also makes it more personal. I do this right in front of them and they remember the moment.

ACTIVITY

Create your own checklist to use when speaking for conferences. Get started with a template at:

https://www.cathyfyock.com/the-speaker-author/

CHAPTER TWENTY-TWO

How to Maximize Back-of-the-Room Sales

You've just given a dynamite presentation. Your audience loves you. How do you maximize the opportunity for back-of-the-room sales? Here are some ideas for making sure you're getting full benefit.

Discuss with the decision maker/meeting planner about selling well before the event. Always check with your decision maker before selling books. You may think that your free presentation gives you the right to sell your books, but the meeting planner may not agree, so have this discussion well before the presentation.

Be careful about combining Q&A with sales time. While offering to answer questions may help bring potential sales to your sales queue, it may also clog the system when an attendee has a lengthy question. Offer to answer questions after the presentation in a one-on-one call; or find a friend or volunteer to help you with sales so you won't miss opportunities to sell. This can be a prime time for gathering leads, especially at association events.

Create a checklist of all the items you'll need to make your book sales go smoothly: signage including the costs of books and packages (plus methods of payment accepted), cash receipts, credit card reader, table for signing, pens for autographing, and name tags, business cards, or post-it notes with the information for the signing.

---

*Create a checklist of all the items you'll need
to make your book sales go smoothly.*

#SpeakerAuthor

If you can bring a staff member or recruit a friend or volunteer to help with sales, bring them a tip sheet with pricing information and other details. You may have one person accept payment, while another ensures that book purchasers wear name tags or have business cards so that books can be easily signed. Some authors have found that having a staff member include a post-it inside the book with the individual's name is a fast way of expediting the line.

Make it easy for attendees to purchase your book. In pricing your book, make it quick and easy. Many attendees come with a $20 bill, so charge $20 and save yourself from making change and holding up the line. Also, bundle products to offer value for attendees.

Accept credit cards by using a card reader. Practice prior to the event, or, better yet, find an assistant to help you with sales so that you can schmooze with attendees and sell more books (and book more engagements!).

Take pictures of you holding your book with those who have purchased your book. Post these on social media and share the post with your new readers.

ACTIVITY

Create your own back-of-the-room checklist for your next presentation. Get started with a template at:

https://www.cathyfyock.com/the-speaker-author/

CHAPTER TWENTY-THREE

Generating More Speaking Assignments When You Speak

There are many ways you can generate more speaking engagements while you speak!

You'll find that many of these ideas are parallel to the suggestions we outlined earlier about sprinkling the narrative of your book with examples about your speaking. During your keynote, workshop, seminar, or webinar, you might include some phrases that let the audience know that you are a speaker and that you regularly provide programs on this and similar topics. While it may seem obvious to you that you would like to do more speaking, the audience may not be aware and are only given this idea when you mention in your presentation that you do other presentations. Do this by including phrases such as the following:

When I was in Dallas last week speaking for XYZ organization . . .

In one of my workshops, someone asked me . . .

One of the problems faced by your industry was voiced when I last spoke with . . .

*Here's a great example that was shared as
a recent program . . .*

Also, be sure your introduction identifies you as a speaker, and perhaps even mentions similar audiences for which you've spoken. Don't assume that your audience will know that this is one of your primary revenue streams!

---

*Be sure your introduction identifies you as a
speaker, and perhaps even mentions similar
audiences for which you've spoken.*

#SpeakerAuthor

In your handouts, include a short bio that identifies you as a speaker. Include contact information on each page. Once Cathy attended a program and wanted to follow up with the speaker some months later, but was not able to find the speaker's contact information (and had forgotten the speaker's name). If only the speaker had made it easier for audience members to find her!

Another strategy for being asked back by decision makers is to ask your audiences what information and programs they need to be successful, what their major pain points are, or what they'd most like to learn in follow-up sessions. Survey your audience members (you can use your response cards or a survey), and then share that information with the decision makers as a next step. It's your job to make sure the decision maker is aware of everything you do.

ACTIVITY

What can you do to be more intentional about generating more business when you speak?

CHAPTER TWENTY-FOUR

Add Aftercare to Your Offerings

Aftercare is defined as "subsequent care or maintenance." When Lois had surgery several years ago, part of her recovery included aftercare. It involved a visiting nurse coming every couple of days to check in and perform any necessary procedures. It got her thinking, *"Why don't speakers offer the same thing?"*

Lois defines aftercare as a follow-up service that helps the client accomplish more than could possibly be done in a single speech.

After your program, make a follow up "thank you call" within 48 hours of the event.

#SpeakerAuthor

Within 48 hours of giving your speech, call the person who made the economic decision to bring you in. Timing is important! You want the great job you did to be fresh in mind. When you connect, here are some topics to cover, and the script:

- I wanted to call and say thanks again for bringing me in. It was a privilege to work with such great people!
- I also wanted to make sure the feedback you heard was as positive as what I heard before I left.
- If you could put some of that feedback in the form of a testimonial I would appreciate it! I'll send you my LinkedIn address, so you can write it in that platform.
- I consider referrals to be the highest compliment. If you can think of anyone who could use my work, let me know.
- Are you a member of an association or trade group? My message would be a good fit there. Can you help get me considered for a program at that meeting?
- Do you think it would make sense (Lois's phrase that pays!) to take a "next step" with me to ensure that the information, tactics, and techniques I talked about are actually implemented? If you do, I'd love to discuss what that might look like. My clients tell me they feel this adds an element of accountability.

If you get voice mail let your contact know that you'll be sending an email to ask for feedback on the event. Put the questions in an email and offer two times you are available to talk.

By "taking the next step" we offer these solutions:

- Do a webinar or series of webinars, or a Skype or Zoom meeting, with key leaders or sales managers that could be recorded and shared if some can't make the meeting.
- Buy books or recordings or other products you may have that support your message.
- Write a series of customized blog posts.
- Record a series of videos.
- Provide one-on-one consulting with key leaders.

"Do you think it would make sense to take an extra step to ensure that the ideas, techniques, and strategies I talked about are actually implemented by your team?"

Lois said this when she was doing sales programs. Interestingly, several times she generated more revenue on the aftercare than she did doing the speech! In fact, many times the speech was more like a paid showcase. Aftercare can be consulting, a webinar, teleseminar, products or even another speech or training. It can be an online sales meeting on Skype or Zoom that is recorded. That way the client can have any manager who may have missed the meeting review the video.

ACTIVITY

Create your own checklist for your aftercare offerings! Get started with a template at:

https://www.cathyfyock.com/the-speaker-author/

CHAPTER TWENTY-FIVE

Response Cards

You also have the opportunity to follow up with the attendees, since each person may be a decision maker for their company or association. Cathy likes to use a response card since so many attendees forget to bring business cards or just don't carry them. Cathy's cards ask for contact information and offer check boxes for the information they would like to receive. One of the best questions on her response cards asks: What group do you know where Cathy would be a great speaker? There is room for that contact information.

Once you have collected the responses, keep in touch with your tribe by sending newsletters, by connecting on social media, or even by offering a special follow-up program or offer for attendees.

In newsletters and on your website, tell your tribe where you're speaking, topics, titles (it gives them ideas about how they could engage with you).

In summary, just because the engagement is over doesn't mean your opportunities to sell more speeches or books have ended.

SPEAKER AUTHOR CASE STUDY

Amy C. Waninger, Network Beyond Bias

If you plan carefully, you can use response cards for more than just gathering contact information! My response cards are the size of a standard post card. I put my contact information (company name and logo, phone number, email address, and more) on both sides.

On the front, in full color, I ask "What's the ONE THING you'll do differently as a result of today's program?" Also on the front are two check boxes: "Yes! Send my complimentary eBook!" and "Yes! Call me to see if I followed through."

On the back, I ask for the audience member's name, company, email address, and phone number. There are also check boxes to request more information about my programs and services.

After each event, I compile all the "takeaways" and send them back to the event organizer, along with a request for a letter of recommendation. It's easy for them to say "Yes!" based on the impact I've had on their organization.

I also take photos of each card's full-color *front* side and post the hand-written testimonials to social media. (Since the respondent's contact information is on the *back* of the card, I can do this without violating anyone's privacy.) My headline reads something like "Do you want to have this kind of impact in *your* organization? Let's talk!" My contact information is visible in each image, so no matter how it gets re-posted, I'll be easy to find!

The Speaker Author

SPEAKER AUTHOR CASE STUDY

Arlene Cogen, Give to Live: Make a Charitable Gift You Never Imagined

Before the Book Is Published

As I was finishing my book, I received a booking to speak for the Financial Planning Association's midwinter conference. I learned from a fellow NSA colleague how he was developing promotional materials to build client lists and promote interest in his book before its publication.

To produce similar materials, I needed my title and book cover. Picking a title and picture for a book in advance of the book's completion was difficult. It took days to find the right title and corresponding image.

The marketing pieces—a book announcement and comment card—included a headshot, contact information, and mock-up, and were used for list building and referrals. Comments produced excellent testimonials for the website.

At the conference, the announcement and comment cards were at every seat. Toward the end of my presentation participants filled out and turned in the comment cards, and I conducted three drawings for autographed copies of my book.

From that event, an investment advisor booked me to speak. Attendees received autographed books.

One month before the book launch, I started sending marketing announcements to my list generated by the comment cards. The announcement had the book cover, a sneak peek, and testimonial. They were sent four weeks, two weeks, and just prior to the book's launch on Amazon. After a week of driving sales to Amazon, I became an Amazon #1 Bestseller.

After Publication

After the book came out in early November, I asked the FPA president if I could deliver the books to the winners from the midwinter conference at their next meeting. At the next meeting, the president spoke about my book and the drawing. He turned it over to me. I thanked the president and called the winners to come pick up their books. There was silence; no one who won the book was there. After the meeting, a dozen advisors came up and purchased the book. The winners received their copies in the mail.

As you can see, here are just a few ways I've cross-marketed speaking and book sales.

ACTIVITY

Plan how you will gather contact information during and after your speaking engagements. Will you use response cards or another strategy? Get ideas and examples at:

https://www.cathyfyock.com/the-speaker-author/

CHAPTER TWENTY-SIX

Creating Your Own Speaking Events

Getting hired by an association or corporate organization is a logical way to begin speaking, but developing contacts and leads, following up, and eventually booking the engagement does take time.

Some who want to move more quickly may want to hold their own public events, which can be short or long programs, live or virtual, single-focused or multi-focused, in-house or public.

Let us first outline some of these options and give you some ideas for implementation.

Morning executive briefings. Morning briefings appeal to executives and busy professionals who can't be away from the office for long. We see many law practices and wealth management companies offering these at no charge to their clients, or others offering these for a nominal fee.

Webinars. Virtual learning events are gaining in popularity as technology becomes more accessible and user-friendly, and individuals have the convenience and comfort of joining from their desks or home offices. There are no physical space issues, which minimizes risks in having to pay for meeting space and is also appealing when reaching out to diverse geographic markets.

Lunch and learns. When delivering information to staff, lunch-and-learn events can be a convenient way to offer bite-sized learning. These may be either in-house events or public events. Attendees may bring their own sack lunches, or lunch may be provided. Lois prefers the term "executive briefings." She feels it's more of a "money term."

Workshops or seminars. If you have more detailed information, you may want to offer a half- or full-day workshop or seminar. When Cathy was beginning her speaking practice as an HR professional, she hosted a one-day program with a colleague, traveling to nine cities over a three-week period. While she didn't make much money for the three-week adventure, she did build her tribe and successfully leveraged future business from her contacts.

Retreats. If your topic warrants it, you may offer a one-day or multiple-day retreat. This format is helpful when working with clients on transformational issues, or when a deep-dive is required. Retreats can be held in corporate settings, or in remote or destination settings. Cathy has held weekend writing retreats for her clients and prospects and plans to add more programs.

Conferences and online symposiums. If you have multiple speakers, you might offer a conference or online symposium. This obviously takes more time and organization but can be a dynamic way to quickly build a following.

With each of these options, there are some pros and cons to consider.

You own the risk—both upside and downside. What if you rent hotel space or a fancy retreat center and no one signs up? What happens when more people sign up than you can

handle? If you are holding the event, you own the risk. Of course, if your event is a huge success, then you will also realize all the benefits.

You own the risk—both upside and downside.

#SpeakerAuthor

You must promote the event and get "butts in seats." Do you know how to reach your target market? Do you know if there is a demand for this topic? Will the topic be approved for your audience to attend and will the cost of the event be approved? Who can you reach out to in order to help you promote your event? All of these are important elements when deciding to launch your own event.

You will need to handle registration and other logistics. Do you have registration software? Do you have the staff necessary to handle registration and other logistics such as booking the venue, ordering food, and offering refunds?

You will need to have a way to move attendees through your pipeline. Even if you have a successful event, the big question is, does it reach the right market to lead to more sales for your pipeline? Consider identifying your next offering after individuals sign up to attend.

Do you charge, and if so, how much? You'll need to gauge what your competition is charging, what the market will bear, and other issues. Do your homework to find the right price point for the level, length, and topic of your presentation.

Obviously, running your own events is a complicated matter. You might find that you can share the risk and reward by teaming up with a colleague who has a similar or complementary topic, or by identifying a sponsor or host who would benefit from the connection. For example, you might team with a law firm that regularly hosts lunch and learns or executive briefings and offer to provide the content for their program.

ACTIVITY

Is it possible for you to hold your own speaking event? Find colleagues who have staged their own events and learn from them. Outline your key ideas.

PART V: POSITIONING TOOLS FOR SPEAKER AUTHORS

As Speaker Authors, we need to be able to communicate to decision makers about the work that we do and sell them on hiring us as their speakers. And, since many decisions about hiring speakers are not made by one person but by a committee, Speaker Authors need to create a variety of tools to communicate topics, value, and other issues. Outlined in Part 5 is a review of some of the basic tools every Speaker Author needs to have to get booked in today's event-planning world.

CHAPTER TWENTY-SEVEN

How to Create a Powerful Positioning Statement

The most important thing you can do for your speaking business or your book is to position it well. In doing so, you must be able to answer the question, "Why hire me instead of someone else?"

Our approach with clients has always been to introduce them to what we call a "positioning statement." We define it as the concept and outcome of working with you. It is the foundation of your business. If you haven't done positioning work first, you may have wasted a lot of time.

You can create marketing plans, materials, and web pages filled with information. However, without proper positioning, none of it is seen in context and it will never be clear.

Lois's positioning statement is an example of concept and outcome marketing: "I work with speakers who want to book more business, make more money, and fully monetize their intellectual property."

Here's Cathy's: "I work with professionals and thought leaders who want to write a book as a business development strategy."

Isn't this more powerful than merely saying "I consult with professional speakers about their businesses," or "I'm a book coach"?

> *If you have a positioning statement,*
> *everything else — all content — must be*
> *congruent with that statement. Every*
> *marketing piece, website, blog post, article,*
> *consulting program, speech, and product*
> *must connect with your market positioning.*

You make your life much easier once you adopt a positioning statement. It's what we say when we network, when we write, when we leave a voice mail, on all of our social media sites, and especially when we do outbound marketing and selling to get clients. A sample call/contact may go like this:

> *Sorry I missed you today. My name is Lois*
> *Creamer. I work with professional speakers*
> *just like you who want to book more*
> *business, make more money, and fully*
> *monetize their intellectual property. I'm*
> *calling to see if ...*

Also, as a professional communicator you should be able to explain what you do in an economy of words. Seven seconds or less. Remember, Speaker Authors, we are in the communication business!

Lois used to do sales programs for corporations and associations under the banner "Fast Forward Selling." She does a few programs a year now for repeat clients.

When reaching out for a sales speaking opportunity Lois may say:

> *My name is Lois Creamer. I work with organizations like yours who want to fast forward their selling skills so that they will be more successful at what they do. I'm calling to see if one of my programs may be a good fit for an upcoming program.*

Every time you call anyone about anything you do, always open with your positioning statement. It's much more powerful than giving your name and a label like speaker, consultant, or author.

Another example of a positioning statement used by a former Army General who now speaks on leadership:

> *I work with leaders who want to stand up, step up, and take charge.*

Believe me, he gets attention!

If you have a positioning statement, everything else — all content — must be congruent with that statement.

#SpeakerAuthor

Other examples:

- I work with organizations that want to develop tomorrow's great leaders today.
- I work with organizations that want to create a workplace environment where employees feel valued, appreciated, and acknowledged.

If you gift yourself with great positioning, you'll reap the rewards of better defining yourself in your target markets. You'll be speaking in the language of "concept and outcomes," and you'll be much better received. You'll open more doors!

ACTIVITY

Type your positioning statement, print it out, and begin using it. Paste your statement on your computer, on your phone, in your notebook—anywhere you may need this inspiration. Now, tweak your statement based on feedback you receive. Rinse and repeat!

CHAPTER TWENTY-EIGHT

Develop a Speaker Author One-Sheet

What's a one-sheet? It's generally an 8 ½ x 11 page that details who the Speaker Author is; what topics they speak about; testimonials from consulting and coaching clients, readers, and audiences; and contact information.

You may be thinking, "Aren't they passé?" Our reply is, "You only need one if you want to speak."

We're very serious about one-sheets and you should be, too. They are still your primary marketing piece that can be used in a number of ways such as:

- Mailer or email to prospect or client
- Follow-up email to prospect
- Information to have on a product table that people can take home
- Handout to leave on attendee seats
- Script for when you are selling over the phone
- One-page marketing piece that can make any agent sound like they know you

We think they are a great exercise in drilling down on positioning and expertise. Your one-sheet can be one-sided or two. Here is the information that should be on the front:

- Business portrait picture
- Positioning statement that describes you and the problems you solve
- Speech titles and bullets that explain the takeaways. Each should begin with an action word
- Picture of the book cover, a short description, and a few testimonials
- Testimonials from clients, readers, and audience members who have heard and love you
- Blurb about your expertise and yourself, although not a long bio
- Social media addresses
- Contact information

If you do a second side, you may consider:

- More testimonials
- Short blog post
- Client list
- QR codes (quick response codes) that contain client list, link to videos, or link to website

As you fine-tune your book description or summary (by the way, you'll need this for many purposes, including your book's profile on Amazon), be sure to include the following:

- What is your thesis statement?
- What problem do you solve for your readers?
- What is unique about your book?
- What features does your book have (e.g., checklists, questions)?

Your short bio should use terminology that shows value for audience members. Some items you'll want to mention include:

- What value do you add to your readers/audiences?

- What problems do you help them solve?
- Which of your credentials directly speak to your audience?
- What personal qualities or experiences create a human connection? For example, do you have hobbies and interests that might help you connect with your audience?

Session descriptions should be catchy and memorable and should identify the value for the audience. The best titles are either your book title or a variation so that your book will be memorable. Be sure to begin each bulleted point with an action verb: develop, create, explore, identify, discover, learn, use.

If you have all of the above on a one-sheet you are golden! Over the years Lois has worked with a couple of speakers' bureaus who have told her that one-sheets are important to them. They use them as scripts just as she suggests. They expect you to have one! Have it available to email and in a PDF file on your website so it can be downloaded. One-sheets make life easier for you and everyone who works with you.

If you would like to see copies of Lois's and Cathy's one-sheets, feel free to email them at

Lois@BookMoreBusiness.com

and

Cathy@CathyFyock.com

Put "email one-sheet" in the subject line. You can use these as templates.

One-sheets are here to stay.

ACTIVITY

Create your one-sheet. Share it with five colleagues and get their feedback. Begin using this as a tool to create speaking opportunities.

https://www.cathyfyock.com/the-speaker-author/

CHAPTER TWENTY-NINE

Your Book's Positioning Statement

A thesis statement appears near the beginning of a written work and offers a concise claim for argument—or a concise solution to the issue being addressed. A thesis statement is best as a single sentence; it can occur as more than one sentence, but it should be distillable to one sentence even if you choose to spread it out.

You should never confuse a topic for a thesis statement. The topic is what you're writing about; the thesis statement is exactly what you're arguing about that topic. The topic is the subject of our hypothetical debate; your thesis is what you actually argue in that debate. If a sample topic is "having dinner sometime," one thesis statement might be, "We should go to Harrod's on Sunday night."

Consider Cathy's book *UnRetirement*. The topic of the book was "the aging workforce," but the thesis was something closer to "Older adults may want to reinvent themselves instead of fully retiring." That's a single, concise argument, and it summarizes the direction of the whole book in one sentence. There's plenty of material to unpack, and plenty of answers that readers might want to hear from those claims, but the whole book is focused on providing exactly those.

The thesis is what gives you direction. Without a thesis, you're writing about something, as opposed to writing something.

The thesis is what gives you direction.

#SpeakerAuthor

Good argumentative writing always has two important pieces. The first is a clear, pointed thesis statement, and the second is a well-organized outline. With those two pieces, you can stay on track with every word you write. In the end, style has very little to do with success, and grammatical correctness almost nothing to do with it (aside from meeting the minimum standard). Do your homework, and you'll be in good shape!

ACTIVITY

Write your thesis statement. Print it. Post it. Continue to tweak it.

CHAPTER THIRTY

Your Magic Button

Cathy often gives aspiring authors a button when she meets them for the first time. When she gives it to them, she explains that it's a magic button. Some laugh or smile nervously when she says that. "It really is a magic button," she says, "but only when you wear it."

The button says Ask Me About My Book!

Ask Me About My Book!

#SpeakerAuthor

The button truly is magical—and we have many clients who will now testify to that magic.

The first bit of magic happens when the author gathers the *chutzpah* to actually put on the button—and wear it in public, where others can see it (and not under a sweater, as one client tried to sneak past Cathy). By wearing the button openly, you set an intention.

"I *am* writing a book," you say to the world. Even that's pretty hard for some aspiring authors, since they really haven't *owned* the fact that they are aspiring authors.

By wearing the button, you also create accountability with everyone who sees you wearing it. Once you wear the button, someone likely will later ask, "How's the book coming along?" and you'll have to provide an answer. It can even hold your feet to the fire as Lois can attest!

But perhaps the button's best magic is its way of forcing you to fine-tune your thesis statement. When asked, "What is your book about?" you will have to state, time and time again, the whole compelling idea in just a sentence or two—in other words, your thesis statement. And you'll get feedback from everyone you tell, whether it's explicit in their words or implicit in their behavior and engagement.

Does the person lean in and ask more questions? Does the person suggest other stories or ideas? Or does the person suddenly need to excuse herself? If the latter is the reaction you receive, you probably have some work to do in reframing your thesis, since it's not yet resonating with your readers.

If after 20 minutes you still can't tell the listener exactly what your book is about—or if you understand what you're saying but the listener seems not to—you have important work left to do. You should be able to tell people precisely what your book is about in 30 seconds, if not well under.

You'll feel the magic when your listener wants to hear more once your 30 seconds are up.

Do you need a magic button?

ACTIVITY

If you have a magic button, wear it to discover its magic powers. You can also receive similar results if you place "Author of the forthcoming book . . ." on your email signature.

CHAPTER THIRTY-ONE

What Should Your Website Say About Your Books and Your Speeches?

We suggest having a website for you as a speaker and author. Many Speaker Authors use tabs to offer a deeper dive on information relating to their books and their speaking businesses.

Lois has a deliberate approach to websites. When working with any client, she creates first a positioning statement and then a one-sheet.

Lois considers a well-crafted one-sheet as a "micro" look at your business, specifically relating your core offerings. In essence, it's the "who, what, when, where, how, and why" of your business. As you approach developing your website, your one-sheet should be your guide.

Consider your website as the "macro" look at your business. Consider that while you have limited space on your one-sheet, you have unlimited space on your website to go into more detail.

---

*Consider your one-sheet as the "micro" look
at your business and your website as the
"macro" look.*

#SpeakerAuthor

Warning! Lois suggests that even though you have unlimited space on your website, you need to measure your words! As a Speaker Author, you must be able to communicate your business using an economy of words (one of Lois's often-used phrases!).

Don't put too much narrative on your site. Break it up, use bullets, sections, action words, and client/audience "takeaways" when describing what you do for clients. Remember – Lois says the reason speakers are hired is to bring some kind of behavior change – new ways of doing things that will increase profits, productivity, and engagement.

A good website for Speaker Authors should be clear, crisp, and compelling. Your "call to action" should be for the prospect to want to talk about what you can do for them.

ACTIVITY

Review your website to ensure that you have the building blocks, and that your one-sheet is congruent with your website content and branding.

CHAPTER THIRTY-TWO

Do You Need a Video Demo?

Your video demo is your proof of performance. It means more to a decision maker than a testimonial or reference (although those are still important) because the meeting planner can see you in action.

Some speakers develop demo videos that introduce the meeting planner to the speaker. They may include a variety of short clips from presentations, studio chats with the speaker, and testimonials from happy meeting planners and audience members.

Some meeting planners and bureaus may prefer to see an entire presentation to determine fit. It's helpful to have a presentation with a live audience for these purposes.

If you are thinking about making a standard preview video, I suggest beginning with your positioning statement. Then have a few self-contained points or stories. Act as your own "master of ceremonies" and introduce each clip.

Make sure your video shows you delivering content within ten seconds. A bureau owner told me this. He said when a video didn't, he pulled it and tossed it. He wanted to see platform time immediately.

At the end, sum it up with an action statement. Something like, "If you like what you see, I would love to work with you!" I suggest you have your video on your website and YouTube.

Many speakers have video clips on their sites. These are great! However, I think a formal preview video is something you should seriously consider. There are experts who can help you put together a terrific one, or you can do it yourself.

If you have a great preview video it will pay dividends!

What if you're a beginning speaker and don't yet have any video footage?

Negotiate for video footage when speaking for free or "when you waive your fee." Since some videographers may charge thousands to create a demo reel, finding good free footage is a great negotiable item.

Negotiate for video footage when speaking for free or "when you waive your fee."

#SpeakerAuthor

Have you presented a recorded webinar or virtual presentation? While it's not the same as having a professionally produced video, it can at least give the meeting planner an idea about how you address your topic and your presentation skills.

Join your local National Speakers Association (NSA) chapter and look for opportunities to create video demos. Cathy's Kentucky chapter has an academy for aspiring speakers, and for "graduation" offers each attendee the opportunity to record a short demonstration with a live (and enthusiastic) audience.

Team up with fellow Speaker Authors and pool resources for a videographer. You might consider a college intern or wedding videographer for a cost-effective option. Gather friends to be audience members to ensure a high-energy presentation.

ACTIVITY

Look for opportunities to get video footage of your presentations, or approach other speakers for their best contacts. Outline what you'd like to include in your demo.

CHAPTER THIRTY-THREE

Products and Other Collateral

When selling back of the room, you may find that having a banner or bookmark will entice audience members to purchase your book.

Banners can be table-top or floor models and can be designed to include the book cover and your photograph. Keep banner design clean and use high-definition images for best results. We like Lisa Braithwaite's banner with a colorful photograph of the author posing with her book, *Presenting for Humans*. The banner identifies Lisa as a speaker and author and provides contact information. She's received positive response for her modest investment.

Client Melinda J. Kelly, Speaker Author of *Finding Your Coach Diving Deep Within,* likes her table-top banner that is super easy for travel out of town. The banner features her book cover, and she can take it to speaking engagements, book signings, and other Speaker Author events.

Bookmarks are easy to create and inexpensive to purchase. Include your book cover and your contact information, plus some ideas or tips from your book's and speech's message. It's better than a business card since it identifies you as an author and is something that audience members tend to keep in their current read. Cathy likes to include a bookmark at every attendee's seat and leaves a stack on the book table.

(Some audience members will prefer to buy the eBook and will use the bookmark as a reminder to make the purchase after the program.)

Bookmarks are easy to create and inexpensive to purchase.

#SpeakerAuthor

Author Jeff Nally uses **postcards** with helpful ideas and tips that also include his contact information and positioning information.

Cathy also uses **response cards** to track follow-up opportunities. Her response cards have space for attendees to print their name, email, and phone, and also ask about the important elements of the presentation and next steps.

In addition to selling books in the back of the room, some speakers find that they can maximize their revenue when they offer a variety of branded **products** to sell, either individually or as a package. Some ideas include:

- Tee-shirts, hats, or coffee mugs branded with a speaker quote
- Plaques or other items suitable for framing with the key points or takeaways
- Branded journals and workbooks

Other speakers have found low-cost trinkets that serve as anchors for key points (for example, a baton when the message is about orchestrating success, or a mini Tabasco bottle as client Brandon Smith, author of *The Hot Sauce Principle*, provides to audiences when he speaks about urgency and change.

One client, Eric Williamson, created "NO Jerk" stickers that participants could purchase after his presentation based on the message of his book, *How to Work with Jerks.*

Cathy likes to hand out her magic buttons that say *"Ask me about my book!"* She loves giving these at conferences to all authors and aspiring authors and creates interest from those who don't yet have a button! These are branded with a small sticker on the back with a picture of her book cover and her web address. She's also added laptop and cellphone removable stickers with the same message, but with a small but readable message pointing individuals to her website.

Some authors create packages of products. For example, Lisa Braithwaite offered her book with a beach bag and other summertime products for her summer reads bundle. Or, you can work with other authors to create a unique package. (Lois and Cathy exchanged boxes of books, which they sold as packages and used as client gifts.)

ACTIVITY

Consider one new item you might offer either for sale or as a way to gain new business and subscribers.

CHAPTER THIRTY-FOUR

Social Media

News about your book and speaking engagements is great fodder for social media. Whether you're on LinkedIn, Facebook, Twitter, Instagram, YouTube, or others based upon your target audience/reader, keep a regular schedule of posts and updates.

Consider this list of ideas to ensure that you are maximizing your exposure:

- Post excerpted articles from your book. LinkedIn is a great place to post entire articles.
- Post media releases about your book's launch events and invite your tribe to attend.
- Announce upcoming speaking engagements asking for attendees to connect with you before your program, or to meet you in the conference bookstore for your signing at the designated date and time.
- Take pictures at your presentations with your book and your audiences and/or book purchasers and post on social media. Cathy loves getting the entire group together for a selfie with attendees holding their copies of her book.
- Relate current news events to your topic and add a comment.
- Share pictures from your book launch parties.

- Encourage participants in your programs to tweet comments about your topic by adding your Twitter handle on your PowerPoint.

Share pictures from your book-launch parties.

#SpeakerAuthor

- Tweet snippets using your hashtag (or create one for your book's title or key message).
- Announce radio, TV, and podcast interviews.
- Create memes using memorable quotes from your book and your speech by coupling these with unique graphics (we like using the license-free photographs on Pixabay.com).
- Create a blog and post links on social media.
- Announce your book-launch parties and other signing events.
- Send your book or chapter to bloggers.

Social media is constantly changing, so look for new ways to add content to get extra followers. For example, Mark Graban, Speaker Author of *Measures of Success*, shares this tip:

LinkedIn now allows you to directly share PDF files. I uploaded my PDF sample material from my book and it has almost 65,000 views.

Cathy and Lois have found that using a regular scheduling tool (Cathy uses MeetEdgar; Lois uses BufferApp) can help in streamlining the process and making it easy to have a steady stream of content.

ACTIVITY

Create a social media posting calendar each week or month.

CHAPTER THIRTY-FIVE

Staying in Touch

In addition to social media and your website, staying in touch with your "tribe" is an important element of getting booked for speaking opportunities.

You can stay in touch through your newsletter, sending articles and posts to your tribe, or just emailing a thoughtful note or reminder.

You can stay in touch through your newsletter, sending articles and posts to your tribe, or just emailing a thoughtful note or reminder.

#SpeakerAuthor

We like this New Year's message shared by client and Speaker Author Rob Campbell, *It's Personal, Not Personnel*:

Happy New Year and thanks to all of you for your time and wisdom last year. 2018 was amazing and I hope in some way I can help you in 2019.

I'm looking to increase the pace of my professional speaking delivering keynotes, breakouts and inspirational speeches to you and your team. I'm booked deep into April with exceptions but looking to schedule speaking opportunities through the remainder of the year. I've attached a short Ted Talk-like speech I did to close out 2018 and my speaker one-sheet is attached. Connect me with other leaders who might be interested!

Wishing you all great success in the coming year. I hope our paths cross.

Make it Personal in 2019!

Rob

ACTIVITY

What can you do to reach out and reconnect with your "tribe?"

CHAPTER THIRTY-SIX

"Look" Your Fee

So, you're thinking about speaking, but how do you know what to charge? Clients who book speakers are looking for some "clues" about your value as a speaker when they look at your experience and credentials. While this list is just a rough idea, it may give you some parameters to consider when thinking about your fee level.

Free: You have limited if any experience; your book isn't out yet; you are unknown in your market; you have no marketing materials.

$500 - $1000: You have some experience in presenting; you have an active blog, or your book is out; you have some exposure in your market; you have a website and a one-sheet.

$1000 - $5000: You have strong experience in presenting and strong testimonials; your book is selling well; you have a website, one-sheet, plus additional marketing collateral (video demo).

$5000+: You are a speaker who is in demand; you have one or more books that are selling well; you have first-rate marketing materials including videos.

When getting started, we suggest that you first determine your experience, materials, and reputation. Listen to other speakers and find out their speaking fees. Practice saying your fee and closing your mouth; often, the greatest resistance to your fee is in your own head. Quote your price to meeting planners and listen for any resistance. When the response to your fee is, "Wow, I thought your fee would be a lot more," then it's time to consider giving yourself a raise!

Practice saying your fee and closing your mouth; often, the greatest resistance to your fee is in your own head.

#SpeakerAuthor

ACTIVITY

Assess your value as a speaker by rating yourself on the criteria above and set your new fee level accordingly.

PART VI: DEVELOPING YOUR CONTENT

In developing your speech you've developed content that can be used in your book. Likewise, if you are writing a book but haven't been speaking, the content from your book can (and should) be used in speaking.

CHAPTER THIRTY-SEVEN

Developing the Scope

Your speech is likely going to be a much more condensed version of your book. If you've read a favorite novel and then go to see the movie, you're likely going to realize that they simplified the plot or the character development, or even eliminated large chunks from the book. Your speech based on your book will likely be similar, in that it can't contain all the detailed information that you've included in your book.

For example, in Cathy's first book on recruitment, *Get the Best*, she offered a short program (45 minutes to one and one-half hours) on an overview of recruiting principles, offering examples from strategies highlighted throughout the book. If she had a full-day workshop she could review much of the book's content, doing a much deeper dive on certain elements.

In Cathy's more recent book on writing, *On Your Mark*, she rarely covers all the content of the book in any presentation since many of her programs are writing workshops with lots of exercises and points of interaction. When handling a Q&A session she frequently touches on topics from throughout the book.

Does your book offer a framework for solving a problem? Does it offer three principles, four strategies, or ten steps? If so, this might be the basis for your shorter presentation. Or, you could select one of these key ideas and do an entire presentation on one aspect of your book's content.

ACTIVITY

The first step is to determine the scope of your presentation. Will it be an overview of the entire book, or an in-depth exploration of one aspect of your book?

CHAPTER THIRTY-EIGHT

Fleshing Out Content

In fleshing out the content for your speech or your book, we love the example that Speaker Author extraordinaire Glenna Salsbury, CSP, CPAE, uses.

Simply being able to see Glenna on the platform is a teachable moment. She has such warmth, such connection, such authenticity. But she shared a formula she has used for years and it really hit home with Lois. She gave Lois permission to share it with you. It's a formula for creating and organizing a speech. Here it is:

P = Point

S = Story

A = Application

Simple, isn't it? What point are you making? Spell it out. Story. Tell me a story that illustrates the point you are making. Make the story one that is meaningful to your audience. Even better, make it a personal story so they can relate to you. Finally, application. *How do this point and story apply to me, the audience member?* Simple formula, awesome result.

It really makes sense. Doesn't it? Point, story, and application! Another advantage of this formula is that it is easy to listen to and follow if you are an audience member. That should always be a goal as a speaker and a writer.

ACTIVITY

Review your book and determine what might be your keynote or short program based on the book. Or, if you're a speaker, scan your content and determine how you'll craft its message for your book.

CHAPTER THIRTY-NINE

Tips for Authors Who Want to Speak

As an author, you should speak at conferences, seminars, book festivals, fairs, and book clubs as a way to market your book and develop a fan base. Here are seven tips for gaining visibility and developing fans!

Tip 1. Don't read your presentation! While it's fine to have notes (as in a keyword outline), don't read your presentation word for word. Your readers want to hear YOU speak!

Tip 2. Speak up! Use your "outside voice" and speak loudly and distinctly. Be sure that, when you mention the name of your book, you say it slowly and clearly. You know your book title very well, but your listeners may not.

Tip 3. Show your passion for your book. Relate to your audience WHY you wrote your book. What is it about this book that speaks to your heart? Share your excitement and enthusiasm because it is contagious.

Show your passion for your book.

#SpeakerAuthor

Tip 4. Tell your story. Stories are powerful vehicles for engaging your audience (and your readers). Sprinkle stories throughout your presentation.

Tip 5. Ask questions and engage your audience. Ask them how your message speaks to them. Ask them about the parts of the book or your topic that engaged them. Have exercises that involve your audience and that allow them to participate in your subject matter. Prepare your discussion questions in advance and pepper your message with exercises or points of engagement throughout.

Tip 6. Let your audience know how to reach you and how to buy your book. Offer a handout or bookmark with contact information.

Tip 7. End powerfully with an engaging story. Leave your audience wanting more from you!

ACTIVITY

Are you utilizing these tips when you speak? Rate yourself honestly on each of the tips.

CHAPTER FORTY

How to Develop a Speech That Sells Books, and a Book That Sells Speeches

To accomplish this, you need to do two things:

1. Give plenty of examples of audiences you've spoken for or client programs you've worked with throughout the book or speech.
2. Offer opportunities for the audience or reader to reach out to YOU so that you can connect and reach back out to them!

Gift-ology, by John Ruhlin is about the art and science of using gifts to cut through the noise, increase referrals, and strengthen retention. Ruhlin beautifully models how to reward and offer value to readers throughout his book.

At the end of many chapters, he invites his readers to go to his website via a special landing page for bonus material. He offers lots of great "irresistible free offers" (IFOs) on this landing page. After giving your name and email address you receive all the goodies he mentions throughout the book: a video of his Brooks Brothers story, cool ideas to show appreciation, a white paper, a checklist, and other gifts.

What are the gifts that you can offer to your readers and audiences? Here is a partial list to get you thinking about all the ways that you might add value for your readers (and, at the same time, get their names and contact information so that you can incorporate these folks into your tribe):

- An assessment, questionnaire, survey, or quiz
- A white paper, eBook, or additional reading
- A resource list or bibliography
- A checklist or template
- An update, newsletter, or brief
- Discounts for future product or service offerings

---

*What are the gifts that you can offer to your
readers and audiences?*

#SpeakerAuthor

- Access to webinars or learning programs
- A podcast or interview
- A video program
- Access to a Facebook or other social media group
- A strategy session with you
- Cartoons or memes with reminders or quotes
- Tweetable content relating to your book

Notice that many of these gifts not only add value to the reader, but they also demonstrate what you might offer to this reader as a client or customer.

Ruhlin closes his book by suggesting that each of us can become a giver-preneur. And as authors and speakers, that is smart business.

ACTIVITY

Create several Irresistible Free Offers (IFOs) based on other materials you already have developed, or which got cut from the book. Use these to encourage your readers to come to your landing page or website to register and receive more goodies, and your audience members to get the bonus materials and remain connected.

CHAPTER FORTY-ONE

Keynote vs. Workshops

Is your speech a keynote, a workshop, or a seminar, or something else? Unfortunately, there is no single definition for any of them. Some consider a keynote to be 45 minutes, others 90. Some call a workshop a half-day affair while others call that a seminar.

Lois has a simple solution: Call them programs! Your program can be a 20-minute presentation, a full day, or longer.

These terms cause so much confusion in the marketplace that even the people who plan the meetings define them differently. This means that you must have the prospect/client define what they need and what they mean. Doing this allows you to make sure you are selling them exactly what they need and delivering within the time frame they request.

A cautionary tale from Lois: A few years ago, she worked with a well-known speaker who shall remain nameless. He promoted himself as a "keynoter" all over his marketing material and his website. Lois and this keynoter worked together to see if she could help him come up with new ideas for growth.

Prior to working together, he sent her all of his material so she could review it. She kept noticing keynote, keynote, keynote. She asked him if when he worked for associations he did any breakouts after his keynote. His reply: "No." Why? "I was never invited to do so." She replied, "And at this rate, you never will be."

She suggested that perhaps they weren't hiring him to do breakouts because he advertised only keynotes. "You're telling them this is all you do, and they believe you." Prospects indeed hired him for what he said he did.

In his materials and website, they changed the wording to "Programs" instead of "Keynotes." It made a difference! It made a difference in the way he talked with his prospects and it certainly made a difference in the way they viewed his expertise. This one seemingly small step increased his bookings.

Cathy suggests that you develop a series of programs based on the content of your book. One might be a 20-minute presentation you could offer for Rotaries, Kiwanis, Elks or Lions Clubs. (Lois calls this 'the animal circuit"!)

Another might be a 45-minute to one-hour presentation for opening or closing a conference. You might also create a one- to two-hour program that you can offer as concurrent conference sessions or half-day in-house programs.

Here's one key idea with which we both wholeheartedly agree: Don't try to squeeze your half-day program into 20 minutes! Don't tell the audience you'll have to cut out important details since "they only gave me 20 minutes," and don't talk at record speed to accomplish the task. Thank your decision maker for the time you have and offer a tailored program based upon that time limit. You might let your meeting planner know you could offer a deeper dive if given a longer time frame, but don't make your audience suffer or turn your audience against the person who hired you!

Don't try to squeeze your half-day program into 20 minutes!

#SpeakerAuthor

ACTIVITY

Take your book's content, and create a 20-minute, 45-minute, and one-hour presentation based upon that time frame. Have these programs ready to go well before your book is launched.

CHAPTER FORTY-TWO

Creating Learning Objectives

In responding to a call for proposal, you'll need to craft learning objectives for your presentation. These will be required if attendees are to receive continuing education credits for attending your program, or to ensure that decision makers' learning objectives are being met for their constituencies.

What is a learning objective? Simply stated, it is what the attendee will learn in attending your program. In fact, many learning objectives begin with, "As a result of attending this program, attendees will be able to . . . "

We suggest that you create compelling learning objectives by using strong action verbs at the beginning of each statement.

#SpeakerAuthor

We suggest that you create compelling learning objectives by using strong action verbs at the beginning of each statement.

Examples might include:

- Create
- Identify
- Plan
- Execute
- Direct
- Lead

Not quite as strong, but still good, are verbs such as:

- Learn
- Understand
- Master
- Teach

Generally, three learning objectives will be required for each program you offer.

For example, in a recent program proposal, Cathy's learning objectives included:

- Identify the key benefits of writing a book
- Create an action plan for writing a book
- Identify tips and strategies for writing the book quickly and effectively

If you have the opportunity to speak with the decision maker, ask what they hope to achieve by hiring you as their speaker. Great questions that help to discover the appropriate learning objectives include:

- Why are you looking for a presenter on this topic? What business issues caused you to call me?
- At the end of the program, what behavioral change do you hope to see in your attendees?
- What are the problems that you hope to resolve by hiring me as your speaker?

- What do you need for this group to know or understand after the program?
- What are the results that you hope to achieve after this program?

These learning objectives can be included on your Speaker Author one-sheet so that decision makers can easily see how you will add value to their organization.

ACTIVITY

For each program you offer, create three learning objectives using strong action verbs, and include these on your revised Speaker Author one-sheet.

PART VII: MORE TOOLS OF THE TRADE

You've written your book and you've developed your program. What are the other elements you should consider to maximize your influence as a Speaker Author? In Part 7 we review how to strategically gift books as a revenue strategy, and how to write additional articles and blogs on your topic to sell more books and book more programs.

CHAPTER FORTY-THREE

When and How to Give Away Books

If you believe that the only way to make money on your books is to sell them, let me share a story about our friend Jeff Nally, author of *Rethinking Human Resources* and *Humans@Work*. Jeff participated in two of Cathy's anthology projects (where 15 authors come together to each write a chapter of one book with all their names on the cover). Jeff decided early on that his strategy would not be to *sell* his books but, rather, to *gift* them!

Perhaps your strategy will be about gifting your book.

#SpeakerAuthor

First, Jeff created a list of his friends, colleagues, and prospects, and wrote a personal message to each recipient. Then the books were beautifully wrapped in color-coordinated tissue and wrapping paper, with a postcard detailing his offerings carefully tucked into his chapter within the book. The books were then mailed to his list.

Within just one week, Jeff booked five paid speaking engagements.

We don't recommend indiscriminately giving away your books in order to book business, but we do believe that Jeff executed this plan flawlessly. Here's what he did:

1. He participated in book projects that allowed him to focus on his expertise and his unique value proposition. In each of Jeff's chapters it was apparent that Jeff had expertise in how to become more human at work using brain-based leadership strategies. His chapters spoke about his experience and highlighted how clients might utilize his expertise.
2. He created a list of his *friends* and contacts who would value the book. Jeff is an amazing connector, and he leveraged this aspect of his strengths to reach out and reconnect with those who might not know what Jeff was currently doing (and, therefore, how the recipient might engage with Jeff). Note that he didn't send his books to a list of strangers or leads; these were individuals who had relationships with Jeff.
3. Jeff used all the strategies as outlined in *Gift-ology*, John Ruhl's excellent book about how to build business by strategically gifting clients and prospects. Jeff beautifully wrapped each book which contained a personal and tailored message, making the gift highly valued by each recipient.
4. Jeff let others know, in a non-salesy way, what he was doing and how other clients were engaging with him. In other words, he painted a picture of how he might work with each person receiving a book.

Another author, Lee Quinn, wrote his book with his business partner Lewis Rudy, *On Your Own Terms: Building a Sustainable, Value-Creating Business,* in which he highlighted their consulting company's process for using the MORE (Master of Reverse Engineering) process.

Their goal was to create a book that would be a highly tailored calling card for their most compatible prospects. His company could not be more pleased with the results.

So, you don't have to sell a book for the book to pay for itself. It can pay for itself many times over when you use smart strategies to book high-ticket engagements.

ACTIVITY

Are there some individuals you might gift with a copy of your book? Create a list and send your book to several and monitor the results.

CHAPTER FORTY-FOUR

The Power of PR

Getting published in magazines and journals, on other blogs, or receiving media coverage in radio and television can be a powerful strategy for not only promoting your book, but also for highlighting your expertise for possible speaking engagements.

To begin your database for media contacts, consider the following action strategies:

- **Collect and read publications in your field of expertise**. Be sure to note each publication's address and other contact information. Note the writing style, length of articles, and other issues. Consider the audience. Write to the publication to request writer's guidelines for submission, as well as a publication schedule indicating deadlines as well as emphasis for certain publications.

- **Meet contacts at trade fairs and exhibits.** Look for magazines, newsletters, and journals exhibiting at conventions and trade fairs. On off-peak hours (when the show is slow, and the exhibitors are not busy speaking with potential customers) approach the booth to determine if they are looking for authors (most are), and request additional information (get a copy of the publication, the business card, and writer's guidelines). For example, Cathy has found the Society for Human Resource Management Annual Conference Exhibition to be an excellent resource for identifying potential magazines within human resources and as a result, has had articles published by many magazines.

Seek out editors and reporters at conferences when you attend.

#SpeakerAuthor

- **Seek out editors and reporters at conferences when you attend.** In Cathy's first year in business, she spoke at an industry human resources conference. At dinner, she exchanged business cards with the gentleman sitting to her left. When she learned that he was an editor for their monthly newsletter, she asked him if he was looking for writers/columnists. He said yes, and for over six years she wrote a regular column for this publication, gaining her added visibility and credibility as well as speaking engagements.
- **Accept media interviews.** When attending or speaking at association conferences and workshop programs, make yourself available to editors and writers. Not only can this provide you with great quotes in prominent publications, but it can open the door to writing assignments.

ACTIVITY

Review your database and begin a media contacts section. Consider the business publications you regularly read, your alumni publications, professional journals, and other resources.

CHAPTER FORTY-FIVE

TED Talks

What is TED?

One of the newer platforms for giving speeches is TED Talks, or short talks (about 18 minutes in length). TED is an acronym for technology, entertainment, and design.

The format is fast paced with 50+ talks typically presented over a week. Presenters (some professional speakers but most are not) and attendees have time to network and discuss what they have heard.

In addition to TED Talks, there are TEDx events. These are described as more of a grassroots movement. There are many more opportunities for TEDx. Each event is coordinated independently.

TED lends its name and a set of guidelines. Local organizers and volunteers do the organizing and production. TED and TEDx programs are held all over the world. There are also a number of spin-offs based on the TED platform. Examples are TED Global, TED Women, and TED Youth.

The TED organization reports that it is always looking for speakers who will inform and inspire. Presenters come from some of the world's most admired companies, product designers, and inventors of cutting-edge products. While they do not pay speakers, they offer benefits for professional speakers. One that is especially helpful is that most of the programs are professionally filmed.

Because of its particular requirements, many speakers chosen to present short talks hire experts to help them make the most of their opportunity. One short-talk expert who Lois often recommends is Hayley Foster, one of the premiere coaches on this specialty platform. This is what Hayley says:

> *To use TED to promote your speaking business, you must be invited or selected to give a talk. This is no small feat. TED is biased against professional speakers. They write in their guidelines that organizers should steer clear of professional speakers. They reason that speakers already have a platform to share ideas, and TED is a place for the general population which does not.*

Personally, I believe this is driven by the fact that many of the methods which drive professional speaking success are the ones that get in the way of delivering an outstanding TED-style talk. Because speakers present for a living, they can be perceived to be arrogant and not easy to coach, disregarding that TED-style is a completely different genre.

One huge benefit of participation in TED is that you typically will get great video to use in your marketing efforts.

#SpeakerAuthor

One huge benefit of participation is that you typically will get great video to use in your marketing efforts. Further, talks are housed on the TED YouTube channels giving you additional visibility.

Hayley adds:

> *Decision makers who care about your topic may want to implement the solutions your talk suggests. Meeting planners are using TED and TEDx talks as audition videos. One short talk can showcase your ability to capture and compel an audience to listen to your great take on something fascinating. For this purpose, five to seven minutes is ideal. You'll be lucky if they watch past two!*

Hayley highlights key points within a talk that may make promotion organic, such as:

- A good idea – Something that you are qualified to share that people really need to know
- Catchy phrase – An intriguing title that can ultimately become "click bait"
- Pull-out quotes – to repeat, or a slide that can become a meme
- "Walkawaytalk" – a "Hayleyism" that describes what people remember and repeat after hearing, may be more colloquial than an actual quote

TED is definitely a different form of presenting. You need to know about it in order to be able to take advantage of it in your business.

ACTIVITY

Create the outline for a short TED-style talk based on your book.

CHAPTER FORTY-SIX

Writing Blogs and Articles: Developing the Topic

Writing blogs and articles based upon your book and your programs will continue to position you as a thought leader.

Don't overlook the most obvious way to write a blog or article, which is to excerpt all or a portion of your book's chapter.

#SpeakerAuthor

First, don't overlook the most obvious way to write a blog or article, which is to excerpt all or a portion of your book's chapter. Look for 400- to 800-word chunks of writing that convey a single topic or issue, add a byline that identifies you and how to reach you, and you're done! Cathy likes to use language like this:

This article is excerpted from Cathy Fyock's book, available on Amazon, *On Your Mark: From First Word to First Draft in Six Weeks*. To contact Cathy about speaking for your group or help with completing your book, reach her at . . .

There are a number of other ways to explore content for a blog or article that will help you book more speeches and sell more books.

The topic on which you spend the most work time. Since the area on which you work is typically an area of strength and expertise, why not develop an article on this issue? Chances are that you have been reading, researching, and working with your clients to solve problems in this area, and can provide information that is timely and real-world oriented. In fact, one of the best ways to find blog and article ideas is to listen to the questions your clients ask you. Lois regularly checks the NSA Facebook page to see what questions speakers are asking and then writes 500- to 800-word blog posts about those questions.

Trends in your area of expertise. What trends do you see in your work? What issues are evolving? What do your clients call you about to ask for your expertise? These are no doubt excellent topics for timely articles.

Controversies in your area of expertise. Do you hold a position that is controversial? Do you have knowledge on an issue that is hotly debated? This topic may also be of interest to potential readers.

New legislation. New laws, regulations, rulings, and interpretations provide an excellent source of article material. By writing articles on these issues you continue to position yourself as a resource in your field.

News that is related to your book's topic. How can you connect your book's and your program's topic to what's happening in the news? If you are an HR professional and there is a new twist in the #MeToo movement, perhaps you can write something that discusses sexual harassment in the workplace.

Seasonal. When we think of September, we think of back-to-school season. When you think about February, you probably think about Valentine's Day. Is there a way to relate your topic to a seasonal issue? If your book is about relationships, then the Valentine's Day theme is an easy connection. If you focus on adult learning, September is a natural. The benefit of seasonal articles and posts is that they can be written in advance and be ready to publish on demand.

ACTIVITY

Create and maintain a list of possible blogs and articles you can write.

CHAPTER FORTY-SEVEN

Writing Blogs and Articles: Narrowing the Scope

Now that you've selected the topic, you must narrow the scope of your article. Consider these guidelines for defining the specific issue and treatment:

- Focus on one element of the topic
- How to's for implementation
- Steps and procedures
- Pros and cons, particularly for controversial issues
- Key ideas, tips, and guidelines for specific activities
- Analogy/metaphor articles

For example, throughout Cathy's work she has provided consultation services on strategic recruitment and has written articles on the following aspects of recruitment:

- Recruiting key labor market segments (on targeting techniques, as well as specifics of recruiting labor market segments such as older workers)
- How to conduct some recruitment activity (such as how to conduct an open house, career fair, or other recruitment event)
- Steps or procedures in tracking or planning for recruitment

- Pros and cons of various recruitment approaches, including more controversial activities, such as telemarketing
- Key ideas, tips, or guidelines for implementing specific activities
- An analogy of how recruitment is like marketing and sales

ACTIVITY

With the list of blog topics and ideas you just created, outline a few key issues and keep fleshing out the content until you're ready to write.

CHAPTER FORTY-EIGHT

Writing Blogs and Articles: Writing

You've done your homework. Now you're ready to write the article. What are the considerations to review as you begin? Some recommendations:

- Refer to the guidelines supplied by the publication. Generally, double-spaced, clean, legible copy is desired, although increasingly, providing articles on disk or via electronic media is requested.
- We've found that articles stand a better chance of getting published if they are well organized and presented in manageable, bit-sized pieces. Editors tend to like headings, key points, bullets, and numbered points to break up the article, making it appealing to the busy reader (and what reader isn't?).

We've found that articles stand a better chance of getting published if they are well organized and presented in manageable, bit-sized pieces.

#SpeakerAuthor

- Your article should reflect the real world, and not an academic or rhetorical approach (unless you are writing for that kind of journal). When Cathy first began writing, she was concerned that her writing wasn't formal or "academic" enough. She was quickly reassured by her editors that most publications and, therefore, most readers wanted real-world approaches in conversational language.

- Provide success stories, examples, and cases. Use your experiences as a practitioner to illuminate your key points and provide enough detail to make the story come alive for your reader. A longer success story or case example might be appropriate as a sidebar.

- Write to the pain of your audience. What are the concerns and issues that cause your readers pain? Outline areas that may be alarming or painful to your reader and provide ideas and recommendations for addressing their concerns.

ACTIVITY

Take one of your blog/article ideas and flesh it out using this as a guide.

CHAPTER FORTY-NINE

Writing Blogs and Articles: Writing Your Byline

You've written a first-rate article. Now it's time to include your byline and picture. As we've said before, we recommend that you have a professionally taken recent photograph as a Speaker Author, and this is one of the many uses of that photo.

Next, you'll want to write your byline. This is NOT a biography or a curriculum vitae. If you include a long, rambling list of your credentials, you can be certain that it will not be published in its entirety. And do you really want some editor who doesn't know you or your work to decide which few words they will include about you, if any?

So, write a short, concise byline. It should be no more than one or two sentences, and, for maximum benefit, should tell readers your name and the **name of your book** (so that they can buy it), **what you do for readers** (how they might engage with you), and **how to reach you** (if they want to engage you for a program or consulting assignment).

Cathy's Byline

*Cathy Fyock is The Business Book Strategist
and works with professionals and thought
leaders who want to write a book as a
business development strategy. She is the
author of* Blog2Book *and can be reached at
502-445-6539 or <u>Cathy@CathyFyock.com</u>.*

Lois's Byline

*Lois Creamer works with speakers who
want to book more business, make more
money, and fully monetize their intellectual
property. She is the author of* Book More
Business: Make Money Speaking *and can
be reached at 314-374-4007 or
<u>lois@bookmorebusiness.com</u>.*

You get the idea. Short. Sweet. And, more importantly, gives
all the necessary information for readers who are interested
in going to the next step to either buy your book or contact
you for speaking engagements or coaching/consulting
assignments.

A Letter from Your Publisher

Dear Article Writers:

First of all, thanks so much for writing content for my publication. Whether you know it or not, you are a lifesaver. My publication needs to be fed content on a regular basis, and you have been great about continuously feeding the beast with meaty content written in interesting and compelling ways.

Secondly, you drive me crazy. I'm a volunteer, and I don't have a lot of time to get my publication pulled together. So I really need for you to follow some basic guidelines, and please don't ask me to bend the rules for you.

Here's what I need for you to know:

1. I have a firm deadline for articles for my publication. Please don't ask me for extensions. It's a deadline. Which means no submissions after the due date.

2. I need for you to follow the word count guidelines. If I ask for a 700- to 800-word article, don't send me an article with 1000 words and expect me to edit it for you. I have no idea what is YOUR most important point, so don't expect me to do your work.

3. Include your byline if you want to get credit for your writing. Don't send me a 250-word bio or introduction and expect me to know what you'd like me to include or exclude. Bylines should be one or two sentences about what you do (or how you work with readers) and how they can reach you.

4. When you send me your article in an email, send me your high-definition photo as an attachment and do not embed it in the article. You lose definition when you embed the photo, and your photo will be grainy and unprofessional.

5. If you have developed artwork you'd like to use with the article, please attach it as a separate email with your photo. Let me know (in your cover email) either that you have created this artwork yourself, or that you have permission to use it.

Thanks for listening to that rant.

Next, I'd like to offer some advice. Since I'm not paying you for this article, I'm assuming that you're writing this in hopes of generating consulting, coaching, or speaking engagements or selling your books. So if you want your article to generate business for you, please write it that way.

Here are some simple suggestions:

1. Be sure to include your byline (see number 3 above). You want to let readers know who you are, what you can do, and how they can reach you. If you want this article to generate book sales, you'll need to let your reader know you're an author. You can do this simply in your byline by using "the author of" after your name. If you don't, you're spending your time on an activity that will never provide ROI.

2. In your article, provide stories and case studies that demonstrate how you've solved problems related to your topic. By showing that you can implement solutions, readers will see the opportunity in reaching out to

you. Don't assume they will figure this out on their own.

3. Weave the benefits of your expertise throughout, but don't be salesy. If your article is too salesy, you'll not only turn off your reader, but chances are you won't get your article published.

OK, I think I'm done. I hope this helps you. It certainly has helped me.

I need for you to continue to write, and I bet that you're looking for ways to generate some spin-off business. This can be a wonderful win-win if we play by the rules.

Signed,

Your Publisher

ACTIVITY

Write your byline, and file it in a handy location so that you can quickly access it when writing blog posts and articles.

CHAPTER FIFTY

Writing Blogs and Articles: You're Published . . . Now What?

Once the article is published, do you sit back on your laurels and wait for the phone to ring? Savvy professionals will leverage the publication of an article in these ways:

- Mail a reprinted article to colleagues with a note, or send an email with a link to the article
- Provide links to your articles on your LinkedIn profile, and provide your article as an attachment to your resume

---

Savvy professionals will leverage the publication of their articles.

#SpeakerAuthor

- Post your article as a blog on your blog site, or serve as a guest blogger for a colleague
- Provide reprints as part of your handouts for keynotes, training sessions, and presentations

- Write companion articles that could be put together in a special report, which might be provided as a marketing tool, or sold as a product offering
- Write companion articles that could become chapters in a book (this is one of the most painless methods of writing a book)

Writing articles can be an excellent way to remind others of your knowledge and expertise in the field and can help you boost your business by establishing your credibility as a thought leader. Begin today by focusing on a topic and starting your research.

ACTIVITY

If you haven't done anything with your most recent blog post, consider this list and do at least one of these activities to gain maximum benefit from your effort!

CHAPTER FIFTY-ONE

What Every Author Needs to Know About Being an Author

You're an author! Congratulations! You are now a member of an elite club, and there are some rules that you need to know now that you're a member. Not that you have to follow all these rules, but some of them will allow you to boost sales and help you fully enjoy the benefits of membership.

When someone buys your book, you are expected to sign it. Yes, at first it seems rather pretentious and awkward, but it's cool to have a book signed by the author. And guess what, you're the author, so sign your book! Think about what you want to say in your autograph. Now that Cathy is a writing coach, her favorite way to sign books is a riff of her book, *On Your Mark*, when she signs, "Make Your Mark!"

Wear your "Ask me about my book" button. If you want to sell books at the grocery store, at your local Panera, or when traveling, wear your button that says, "Ask me about my book." We guarantee that someone will ask, and if you respond in an upbeat and compelling way, you'll sell books everywhere you go. We also like Cathy's new removable stickers for cell phones and computers with the same message.

Carry at least one book with you at all times. If you're wearing your button and people ask you about your book and want to buy it, it would probably be smart to have a book with you that you can sell! If you're speaking, be sure to hold your book and read from it. You'll create additional interest and potential sales.

Carry a box of books in your car. When you wear your button, from time to time you may have the opportunity to sell not just one book, but multiple copies (but only if you have them with you). Most authors I know are always ready with a box full of books in the truck of their car.

Celebrate the release of your book with a launch party with friends, family, colleagues, and clients. Especially with your first book, your friends have been hearing you talk about this book forever, so for heaven's sake, invite them to your party so they can celebrate with you!

Put your book with a picture of the cover on your email signature.

#SpeakerAuthor

Put your book with a picture of the cover on your email signature. It's a great reminder for clients and prospects to know that you're now an author and a member of this elite club. And who knows, someone may just decide to go to Amazon and buy a copy or two.

Include your book on your website, your social media profiles, and your bio and intro. Let everyone know about your membership in the author's-only club. You may also want to include a link to Amazon so that interested individuals can quickly and easily make purchases.

Get your 30-second commercial down cold. What is your book about? You should be able to answer this question in your sleep. Figure out what is your most compelling pitch and keep tweaking it.

Look for news events that provide a hook for your topic. What issues and controversies in the news are related to your topic? Continually look for links and be prepared to write blogs and articles on these topics or pitch your story idea to the media for PR opportunities.

Own the fact: It's a big deal! Don't even try to downplay it. You've written a book. That's pretty darn impressive. Own it.

ACTIVITY

Are you fulfilling your role as an author? Explore this list to ensure you're living up to your new role!

CHAPTER FIFTY-TWO

Think Like a Marketer

Kate Colbert, founder of Silver Tree Publishing and author of the acclaimed book *Think Like a Marketer: How a Shift in Mindset Can Change Everything for Your Business*, has advised dozens of speakers and business professionals during their book-authoring ventures. She emphasizes how to write and publish a book that sells, and how to build and embolden author brands. She explains, "A well-written and well-marketed book can allow established professionals to reach a broader audience and redouble the impact of their mission. It expands the possibilities for passive revenue through royalties and it, quite simply, gives authors and organizations the credibility they seek. A professional bio with the words 'Author of …' will always turn more heads."

Kate is our colleague and friend, so we asked her to share some of her secrets — some of the guiding principles that helped her write, publish and promote her own book to help it debut in the top 1% of all business marketing books on Amazon. Here are 7 of the savvy choices she made:

1. Clarity first. Kate was crystal clear on her goals, her priorities, and the audiences she wanted to serve. She engaged Cathy as her book coach on the very day she began writing the book's outline, and used the strategy document that they developed together as her guidepost throughout the eight months she was writing and editing the book. "I didn't have to write a book proposal, per se, but I did it anyway," Kate said. "And I shared it with as many people as would read it, to ensure I was planning a book that others thought was valuable, viable, and authentic to my areas of expertise."

2. Own the timeline. Kate worked like a fiend to produce her 61,000-word manuscript and the marketing ecosystem that supported it. She committed to produce her book with an aggressive timeline but refused to "rush to failure," as many authors do when the deadlines are looming and they're feeling tired. As she said from the stage during a presentation at NSA Influence, "Many business authors release a book the way other people put out the trash. They just want to be done with it and get it out the door before it starts to stink." When it became clear that she was running tight on time — that, in order to meet her self-imposed July 1st release date, she'd have to release a book that was "good, but not great" — she stopped the proverbial presses. She put the book up on Amazon for pre-order on July 13th and had all the key marketing (like the book website,

www.thinklikeamarketerthebook.com

social media pages, and promotional postcards) circulating by the time she took the stage at NSA on July 15th. "Having the book in time for my NSA debut was an ambitious and important goal, but speeches come and go, and this book was going to be forever. I wasn't going to let it be anything other than the best book I could produce." In the end, the book released in paperback on August 25th, eight weeks past the original "deadline" and as an eminently stronger book than what would have been printed in early July.

3. Invest in yourself. From the moment she decided to write *Think Like a Marketer*, Kate treated herself like a celebrity. Why, she pondered, would someone pay her $20,000 for a keynote speech or $100,000 for a market research project if she wouldn't likewise invest in her own brand? So she cut no corners when it came to photo shoots and marketing materials, launch events, and even brand consulting with bestselling author Rory Vaden and his team at Brand Builders Group. "There's no 'return on investment' without, first, the right investment," she explains.

4. Don't cut corners. Too many authors publish a good book with a bad cover, or great insights on cheap paper. Or they get to their release date and are too tired to actually promote the book. Kate insists there's no such thing as too much, if it's authentic and tied to your goals. Kate rallied all the resources of her publishing company, did the hard work of collaborating with editorial board members, hired a great publicist, and engaged 140 people on a "book launch team."

5. Forget the bucket list. Sure, writing a book is about you — about your brand and your business goals. But no one, except your most loyal clients and friends, is going to buy a book if it's not written in service of the reader. Kate attempted to write the book that the marketplace wanted and needed. She used decades of professional experiences with clients to know what lessons they craved and what insights would help them achieve the most remarkable results. She structured the book to provide bite-sized predictions of the future, reader-application challenges in the form of "Ask Yourself" questions, and 5 overarching principles to tie the book together in a way that would be powerful and memorable for readers. During her third and fourth revisions, she added sections — like tips for direct sales professionals — that became fan-favorite sections, and cut major portions of content that didn't test well with early readers. Kate advises that speakers and authors, like all business professionals, "Live and Die by Your Customer Insights." She asks, "What does your customer data tell you about the needs and interests of the people you serve (the very same people who represent would-be readers of a future book you might write)? Are they struggling with topics you could explore in a book? Do they need a go-to resource or framework for their thinking, and are you the best person to write that book?"

6. Escape the distractions. Hard as it is to do, great authors create space for the kind of "deep work" that Cal Newport writes about in his acclaimed book about focusing in a distracted world. "My book is, without doubt, the very best work of my career," Kate says. But she's confident that she couldn't have written this book to her standards had she not regularly done what few authors do. She went into frequent "writer's exile" at a local hotel, skipped family parties in favor of writing all weekend, and wrote on planes, trains, automobiles, and cruise ships. She dictated portions of the book into a voice app on her smartphone, from bed, from the grocery store, and from wherever she was when a good idea struck. She became acquainted with the "Do Not Disturb" feature on her cell phone and her out-of-office responder on her email. When she was writing and editing, everything else had to wait.

7. Know you'll sell more books if it's not all about selling books. Everything about the creation and release of Kate's book was a case-in-point of the book's "Think Like a Marketer Principle #1" — Communicate for connection and meaning, not just to transact sales. When deciding what to write, what to cut, and what to improve, Kate kept asking herself questions like "How can this book help me connect to others in a way that is meaningful for them?" and "Can my book deepen conversations with clients and prospects, create a platform of followers, and allow me to share insights that can inspire solutions for the business problems faced by my readers?" Once the book came out, Kate used the book to connect more deeply to her current clients, making it required reading for her coaching and communications workshop clients, offering guided book clubs for client

175

companies who want help applying the book's principles to their projects, and delivering no-cost speeches (on the sage advice of Lois!) to colleges, universities, and healthcare organizations where Kate was looking to open doors and close deals.

CHAPTER FIFTY-THREE

The National Speakers Association

First, our disclaimer: Both Cathy and Lois are members of the National Speakers Association. What's more is that both are enthusiastic fans of this group!

So, having said that, we still want to emphasize how important we believe this organization is for aspiring and seasoned professional speakers.

Some of the benefits of being a member include:

A place to see "the best of the best." Cathy believes that it is easy to become enamored with your success, and rely too heavily on your evaluations. "When you get evaluations that are four-star, it's hard to see how to improve, or even why to improve. Hanging out with excellent speakers is a way to see your competition firsthand, and to witness the trends in the industry. For many, it's the only place that really "gets" what you do for a living!

A place to up your game. It's easy to become complacent when working solo, and that's another reason that being with other speakers gives you an idea about how YOU can become a stronger, more credible presenter.

A way to see a bigger vision of what you can become. Again, working solo can be limiting. You only see what is possible given your own vision of success. When you're rubbing elbows with other speakers, you understand what is possible and how to play bigger as a speaker and author.

A community of like-minded individuals. As a solopreneur, it's great to have a community of people who get you. When Speaker Author Cara Silletto (*Staying Power*) attended her first annual convention, she called her husband and tearfully commented, "I've found my people!"

NSA is a place to up your game.

#SpeakerAuthor

A community to share best practices. Why should you reinvent the wheel? If others have learned about best practices, isn't it smart to shorten the learning curve and benefit from their experiences?

A place to learn and grow. Where else can you learn about the business of speaking than at the National Speakers Association? You'll learn not only about how to eloquently deliver content, but also about the elements of running your business, leveraging your expertise, and doing it all with the highest of ethical standards.

There are local chapters of the National Speakers Association across the United States; visit NSA's website to find a chapter near you.

https://www.nsaspeaker.org/

If you're serious about being a speaker, you should definitely attend and see if it is exactly what you need to accelerate your speaking career.

ACTIVITY

Go to the NSA website and find your local chapter. Reach out and put the next meeting date on your calendar. Or better yet, plan to attend the next annual convention.

https://www.nsaspeaker.org/

CHAPTER FIFTY-FOUR

Your Call to Action: Change the World

Speaker Authors make a difference. We change the world, one word at a time.

Nonfiction authors and speakers write books and speak about innovating human resources, creating positive organizational cultures, helping poorly performing schools, raising awareness for Post-Traumatic Stress Disorder (PTSD) and Military Sexual Trauma (MST), helping individuals navigate their careers, leading meetings that matter, building confidence for women, using powerful questions, developing a deeper faith, coaching and developing others, supporting a spouse through terminal illness, using positivity to achieve major life goals, working through forgiveness, presenting for humans, and empowering leaders. They also help us learn how to see the holy in the humdrum, live richer and fuller lives, create compassionate organizations, and network beyond bias. That's a lot of good that is going out into the world.

And think of the impact of 100 authors and speakers. If each author distributes just 100 books, and each one of those books has a positive impact on the reader, then 10,000 people are impacted. If one person's 100 books on leadership help improve not only the business but also the lives of the people working for that organization, that impact is further magnified. And on and on the impact goes.

Margaret Mead said, "Never doubt that a small group of thoughtful, committed citizens can change the world. Indeed, it is the only thing that ever has."

#SpeakerAuthor

Now, consider that if each Speaker Author's message goes out into the world 1,000 or more times, then the impact of 100 Speaker Authors is greater still.

Margaret Mead said,

"Never doubt that a small group of thoughtful, committed citizens can change the world. Indeed, it is the only thing that ever has."

We expand upon her quote and say,

"We celebrate the impact of authors and speakers. We are changing the world. One word at a time."

ACTIVITY

We challenge you to make a commitment to change the world!

ABOUT THE AUTHOR

Cathy Fyock

Cathy is The Business Book Strategist and works with professionals and thought leaders who want to write a book as a business development strategy. *The Speaker Author* is her ninth book. She also has been the editor for a series of anthologies focusing on HR, organizational development, and leadership strategies, and has completed nine anthologies, including her most recent, *Imagination@Work*.

In addition to her work as a book coach and author, she is a speaker, enthusiastically helping thought leaders who want to write their books.

She lives in Louisville, Kentucky, with her husband of more than 40 years, Jim.

For information on her one-on-one coaching, speaking, and other services, please contact Cathy at:

Cathy@CathyFyock.com

502-445-6539

http://CathyFyock.com

Connect with Cathy:

https://www.facebook.com/TheBusinessBookStrategist

https://twitter.com/CathyFyock

https://www.linkedin.com/in/cathy-fyock-973b735/

https://www.youtube.com/user/CathyFyock

Also by Cathy Fyock:

Blog2Book: Repurposing Content to Discover the Book You've Already Written

On Your Mark: From First Word to First Draft in Six Weeks

Hallelujah: An Anthem for Purposeful Work

The Truth About Hiring the Best

The Hiring Source Book

UnRetirement

Get the Best

America's Work Force Is Coming of Age

ABOUT THE AUTHOR

Lois Creamer

Lois Creamer is an industry expert working with speakers who want to book more business, make more money, and fully monetize their intellectual property. She is the author of *Book More Business: Make Money Speaking.*

Clients include *Chicken Soup*'s Jack Canfield; bestselling author of *The Sales Bible* Jeffrey Gitomer; Chairman of *C-Suite* Jeffrey Hayzlett; presentation guru Patricia Fripp; and more.

Her expertise and no-nonsense style have led her to be invited to speak at over a dozen National Speakers Association annual meetings, NSA winter meetings, and chapters. She has also presented at Canadian Association of Professional Speakers conventions and chapters as well as Global Speakers Association events.

Lois works with speakers in the areas of positioning, selling, social strategies, and product creation. Prior to *Book More Business*, Lois worked in sales and marketing for the United States Steel Corporation.

Publications in which Lois appears include:

Forbes

Bloomberg Business

Speaker Magazine

The Wall Street Journal

For more information on her speaking and consulting programs please contact Lois at:

Office: 314-374-4007

Email: lois@bookmorebusiness.com

Connect with Lois at:

https://www.Facebook.com/LoisCreamer

https://www.twitter.com/LoisCreamer

https://LinkedIn.com/in/LoisCreamer

https://www.youtube.com/BookMoreBusiness

Made in the USA
Lexington, KY
04 July 2019